SETTING APPOINTMENTS IN THE SMARTPHONE WORLD

SETTING APPOINTMENTS IN THE SMARTPHONE WORLD

GAIL B. GOODMAN

ISBN: 979-8-218-07507-1

Author photo provided by author.
Cover design and layout by Ashish Joshi
Cover layout prep by LACreative.
Cover photo provided with permission by Dreamstime.
Inside pagination by Win-Win Words LLC.

Printed in the United States of America

*To my husband, **Don**, for his unwavering support, cheerleading and pride in my work.*

CONTENTS

SETTING APPOINTMENTS IN
THE SMARTPHONE WORLD

CHAPTER 1
DIGITAL VS. IN-PERSON

I HAVE SPENT THIRTY-PLUS YEARS HELPING FINANCIAL ADVISORS and insurance agents schedule appointments with new prospects and existing clients. In that time, there have been numerous technological and cultural changes involving telephones. The first "technological" change was Caller ID. Then we dealt with a "Do Not Call" law, which traumatized many folks. But the most important innovation, by far, was the smartphone. This little "rectangle" has changed the way we live our lives—and the way we build a professional practice. It has also affected the way we schedule appointments by phone.

Over the last two-plus years we have experienced a devastating pandemic. During that time, many of us have been unable to conduct face-to-face appointments. It is still the norm for some of us and might be that way for the foreseeable future. This has all made phone usage that much more important. Luckily, video software allowed us the opportunity for virtual appointments. The ability to see clients and prospects "in person" was a lifesaver. And now virtual appointments are the norm. The in-person, face-to-face appointment still exists, but the convenience of virtual meetings (for both the professional and client) has made our workday more efficient.

There are language and script modifications that accompany this dramatic transformation. As I've reminded my advisors, **language changes!** We must always use modern phrases to reflect the society in which we live.

My goal has always been and will continue to be helping financial professionals and insurance agents gain new business. When I speak to managers, they always say, "If I get my folks in the door, they're terrific. We have a high closing rate." And I have always responded with the same answer: "That's the easy part." Prospecting is hard.

Let's face it, Americans don't like to talk about money. We don't provide financial literacy training to young adults prior to their going to college and taking on massive debt. We don't teach children how to save, spend wisely, or learn how money grows. Our culture says that money is a taboo subject, a tradition that leads to financial illiteracy. It also presents problems for the financial professionals trying to get everyone to talk about their finances.

Because of this unspoken rule, financial advisors need to be careful how they introduce themselves to prospects. I have been forthright about my feelings that "elevator speeches" are not a good idea. Being in a misunderstood profession requires a different set of words other than "Hi, I'm a financial advisor." It might work better if you're a doctor..

A financial career has a long learning curve. There's a lot to learn! The industry has done a great job of teaching the products, the sales process, and how to create an appropriate financial plan. It has *not* done a great job of helping advisors **build a practice by finding new prospects and getting in the door.** That's where I come in.

Every face-to-face appointment is an opportunity to help someone to be smarter with their money, feel a sense of true financial security, and plan for their future in a more comprehensive, intelligent way. If you can convince someone to sit with you and talk about their finances, you are more than 80 percent of the way to getting them to those goals.

We live in a society where digital communication reigns. Therefore, it is more important than ever to be precise in all your communication, both digital *and* verbal. Many financial companies have strict rules about texting. I disagree with those that ban *all* texting, but I also see some of the crazy stuff being texted from the phones of advisors. I understand why the compliance department is trying to maintain control. But to remove texting from *anyone's* professional life is like sending someone into a nuclear war with bows and arrows. We need to communicate digitally, but in a professional, limited manner. I aim to provide that professional language for you here. And despite the frequency of digital communicating, your verbal skills count just as much.

This book does not claim to be completely in sync with your own compliance department, so be sure to follow their rules.

A Word About Compliance

The financial services industry is highly regulated regarding appropriate scripts and what you can and cannot say on the phone. Many of the included scripts have been approved by most of the major insurance companies I work for, but I include the following disclaimers:

1. **I do not present this book as totally compliant with the rules of any particular insurance company.**

2. **Any agent/advisor using this book as a guideline must get approval from his/her own compliance department and/or manager prior to using any of the scripts or answers to a prospect's responses.**

CHAPTER 2
TALKING vs. TEXTING

THERE SEEMS TO BE A NEW, UNWRITTEN RULE IN OUR SOCIETY. Talking has taken a back seat to digital communication. Let's face it; texting is a quicker way to send a short message—e.g., "I'm running ten minutes late." So we routinely rely on this medium.

The problem is that financial services is a high-trust, heavily regulated industry. Do not assume people will trust you with their money if you completely rely on digital communications. People need to hear your voice as well.

There is a distinct struggle in our world between the texters and the talkers. Your preference isn't what matters. My assertion is that the sound of a human voice trumps a digital message every time. Let's face it—there isn't a single person who hasn't sent, or received, a misunderstood text. That usually happens because it lacked inflection, which only a human voice can provide.

One time after a day-long workshop, I was scouring my emails when I was startled by one from a close friend. It "read" in an abrupt and rude manner, which was inconsistent with our relationship. *Because I knew her well, I understood it was a simple error of word choice.* Instead of getting offended, I immediately called her and asked what she was trying to say. My story had a happy ending. My friend re-explained (this time on the phone, of course) what she was trying to say and our relationship remained intact.

The problem with this scenario is that when you are trying to create a new relationship, or nurture a relationship that is not yet firmly established, a simple miscommunication can cost you. A lot. Like the entire relationship. Or a sale.

This is the problem we are facing on a daily basis. Actually, make that hourly. **All digital communication has the capacity to be misunderstood**. And in your professional life you cannot take the chance of losing a client or referral because your choice of words was inaccurate.

Financial advisors handle confidential information all day. This makes them mindful of what they say and write due to the sensitive nature of their work. But when it comes to prospecting, I do not see a similar caution.

Building a professional client relationship is different from making a new friend. There needs to be a high amount of trust on the part of the client—trust in the advisor's intelligence, integrity, and ability to communicate. There is little room for error.

By choosing to prospect more often in person, you can add a critical communication element—body language. There are many experts who say that as much as 93 percent of face-to-face communication is nonverbal. So why would you remove that advantage from your prospecting activities if you have a choice?

I'm not about eliminating digital communication. Not at all. But when I hear that people are texting and emailing my phone scripts—which are *specifically* designed to be implemented, in real time, with your voice—I know we are in dangerous waters. Too many advisors are trying to create relationships and appointments solely through digital means. That's a huge mistake.

Talking vs. Texting

Being a good talker is important in life. In financial services, it is critical. Besides attaining the initial appointment, your ability to talk about complex products so clients fully understand how their money is being spent is profoundly important. Good talkers are usually better advisors for this reason. And their talking skills are my sole focus!

I teach advisors and managers how to better manage the activities that lead up to a first appointment. Once you have a confirmed initial appointment—i.e., someone willing to sit and talk to you about their financial life—you have moved into "sales territory."

Then I am done.

CHAPTER 3
PEOPLE NEED PEOPLE

WHATEVER YOU MIGHT HAVE DONE IN THE PAST about prospecting, or were considering doing in the future, everyone's life was changed between 2020 and 2022. Some people experienced tremendous loss—of loved ones, their businesses, their money, or their sense of security and happiness. The more we ignore the trauma of the pandemic, the less successful we will be. It does not mean you need to become an unlicensed psychiatrist for your clients and prospects. But a little more empathy, patience, and human kindness will go a long way.

We have not "gotten out of" the pandemic so easily. We are all still reeling from being in lockdown, being isolated and unable to go about our lives in any normal sense of the word. I know many advisors who took the time to reach out via text, email, or phone to reassure their clients. That was wise.

Luckily, we had, and still have, software that allows us to conduct virtual meetings. Later I will address virtual meetings specifically in more detail. Having the ability to see each other on a screen improved our sense of being connected during a very "unconnected" time. We dodged a huge bullet by having virtual software at a critical time in our lives.

Unfortunately, the downside of virtual appointments is that by becoming the norm for so many months, it is now the "go to" choice for many advisors and managers. I, too, am grateful to have been able to continue my work via Zoom. But I am also aware that my Zoom training presentations have huge limitations compared to my in-person workshops.

Here's an interesting example: I worked extensively with a wonderful agency throughout the many months of the pandemic. We did a lot of virtual training. My program included training the managers, conducting four seminars for the advisors, and supervising two role-playing sessions. All went very well and there was a lot of positive feedback. In February 2022, I was asked to speak at their local National Association of Insurance and Financial Advisors (NAIFA) conference and was able to see some of the advisors and managers in person. Right after my live presentation, which was similar to one of the video classes I had conducted for them, the trainer said to me, "Well, now we have to get you into the agency in person."

And that's my point.

As much as the webinars were helpful, there is no substitute for a live teacher. Ask your children. The entire educational system in America was a mess during the pandemic. Living in a more rural (i.e., limited internet) area of Tennessee, I know parents who had to sit in parking lots to access Wi-Fi so their children could participate in their classes. Not everyone had high speed fiber-optic connections during COVID, creating havoc for many. Even those kids with better access often found it hard to concentrate on what the teacher was saying. Teenagers experienced higher levels of depression than ever before. There is a huge amount of blame we can put on social media, but we must also acknowledge that for two years—a long time in the life of a young person—teenagers were isolated from their friends. Nothing matters more at that age than being part of a group. People, especially teenagers, need people,.

Adults like to think they're immune to all of this. We are not. The post-pandemic mental health crisis we are experiencing is widespread. Talk to friends who had rarely been depressed or "blue" in their lives. During COVID many felt unpleasant feelings and moods with which they were unfamiliar.

All of this tells us that the experience of not being with other people was not always so successful.

Here's a simple Rule of Being Human: Someone has to know you before they trust you. The required level of interpersonal trust in a client relationship varies depending on whom you're thinking about. It also makes a difference in how loyal and committed the relationship will become. Trust adds to relationship longevity as well. This is vital for professionals in the financial sector. I don't need to trust my lawn care guy as much as I trust my advisor. I *do* need to trust my doctor and dentist, but not my dry cleaner as much.

Financial advisors are looking to create high trust and long-lasting relationships with their clients. Which brings me to the main point. **More time spent meeting people in person is important for financial service professionals.**

I coach a group of newer advisors at one of my favorite agencies. During a conversation about the value of virtual meetings, a young advisor spoke up, saying he believed that virtual appointments were much more convenient than in-person meetings for both client and advisor. He could not imagine why he or anyone else would ever bother to drive an hour or more each way for an appointment.

In hearing this, I had to work very hard to control my facial expression because we were all on camera. I strongly disagreed with this new advisor, but I also knew that he had been hired during the pandemic. He had not experienced many, if any, in-person appointments. He had not seen the magic that could happen when face-to-face with a new client.

My hope is that by now all "pandemic recruits" have moved into face-to-face appointments exposing them to the level of rapport that can be built when doing these. Experienced advisors always tell me their clients will talk more freely about their money when you're sitting in their home. We can't ignore this fact.

My sales life started out with selling kitchen refacing. It was in its infancy and not as well-known as it is now. I had the privilege of being trained by a fantastic mentor who strictly orchestrated my voice, my body language, when I would stand or sit to make a point and, of course, what I would say. Having been taught by someone who understood the power of body language and precise verbiage influenced my sales career. It has carried into my own teaching methods.

My consulting practice includes workshops that last a few hours. Like my mentor, I work to make sure that any theory I'm teaching on is understood, then practiced. I see the "I got it" moments when we are together. On virtual meetings, I only see slides. Being primarily virtual affects the way I teach, so I suspect it affects how well my students understand what I am telling them. It saddens me to know what they might be missing.

Financial concepts are not easy for most consumers to understand. That is why we need financial advisors to be on a campaign to meet as many people as possible. It is far better to be in person with a client when you need to clarify a complex concept than to explain it via Zoom. Most people agree with me.

If we know all of this to be true, how can we begin the relationship on a better note in the first place?

My answer: Re-think your prospecting and marketing strategies.

Before we get to marketing ideas, you need to ready yourself in a couple of ways. The first is by creating a Digital Business Card. The second is to re-think making random calls vs. scheduling Phone Dates.

CHAPTER 4

USE A DIGITAL BUSINESS CARD

W E CAN ALL AGREE THAT MOST PEOPLE DON'T PICK UP random calls, therefore it is critical to be recognized by the owner of a phone when you make a call. This creates two big rules for you:

1. Have a Digital Business Card.

2. Share your card with everyone you might ever want to speak to again.

Most people keep a personal contact of themselves in their phones. A Digital Business Card is a more professional version of the same thing. It is another contact of yourself with critical business information added.

Here's an obvious fact: The smartphone has forced new behaviors. Most folks ignore calls that only show a phone number. Therefore, you want to be a name and a number that show up on the other end when someone glances at their ringing phone. You *must* be a contact or they will never pick up. The lack of a name makes the difference.

There are some people, and I know a few, who won't accept any phone call. These are people who **will not talk** on their smartphones and only communicate digitally. That's a huge challenge when you're part of a highly regulated industry. Let me be clear. You cannot violate the compliance rules of your company.

It's possible that your ability to reach out to a specific person in a professional and compliant manner is being thwarted by someone who has decided their life is only about texting. If you have an opportunity to meet them in person, that's great. Sometimes you need to just let this person go—or you might put your license at risk.

Do not text your appointment-setting script. I know many advisors who disagree with that rule of thumb and have made appointments by simply texting the content of what I consider an out-loud-in-real-time-only script. But they have crossed the Rubicon of both my rules and those of their respective compliance departments.

Your main prospecting rule is to never, ever walk away from a person without leaving your Digital Business Card in their phone. Being in someone's phone makes you more real to them.

You want to represent yourself professionally in that other person's phone. Therefore, I want you to create a Digital Business (DBC). As mentioned before, it is a professional version of you—not a standard contact. There are specific components that need to be included, so make sure to follow the eleven steps I'm about to tell you.

Once you have a Digital Business Card, you need to be able to share it quickly and professionally. There are two ways to do that. You can create a standard text that has your contact attached, or you can take the time to create a shortcut on your phone. A shortcut would be a custom colored button on the first page of your smartphone. This button will create an empty text with your DBC attached and is ready to be texted to the other person. Make sure to do the same with the other person's information—get it in your phone.

Some advisors have created a QR code that is their Digital Business Card. That is another great shortcut. A friend of mine is a designer, and her standard paper card has a QR code that makes it easy for people to get her into their contacts in seconds. In a digital society, you need to be skilled at smoothly sharing your contact. For the sake of your own professional ego, you don't want to be fumbling with your phone, trying to figure out how to do this process. It should take a few seconds, at the most. Practice until you get it.

Create Your Digital Business Card

Open up an empty, new contact in your phone.

People often remember your profession, not your name. That is why I prefer your title at the top—it should include the word "financial," or "insurance" if you are a property and casualty agent. Some advisors take the time to change the form and add a fourth line at the top of the searchable section. Others solve this problem by putting their first and last name on the *first* line, their company name on the *second* line, and their title on the *company* line. All of those components (above the four other buttons on an iPhone) can be searched. Be thoughtful about which information is there.

Now for the eleven steps I promised earlier. Insert the proper information in the following fields:

1. **Your First Name**

2. **Your Last Name**

3. **Your "searchable" title (i.e., you need the word "financial" on this line)**

4. **Your cell phone number**

5. **Your office phone number**

6. **Your business email (not your personal gmail or yahoo email)**

7. **In the address section:**

   Company name (not after your last name above) I prefer your company name here instead of above

8. **Second line: Street address**

   Third line: City

   Fourth Line: State, Zip Code

9. **Social Media : Your whole LinkedIn URL**

10. **Social Media: Your URL page from your agency website or your own website**

11. **A good photo of yourself—smiling, in professional clothing. No children, animals, funny hats, etc. Just you.**

Once you have a Digital Business Card, you will never need or want to use your paper ones again. Professionally, your job is to get into people's phones. Paper cards get forgotten, stuffed into drawers, thrown into boxes with a hundred others, etc. This contact will, hopefully, help you to get the other person to pick up when you call.

CHAPTER 5

PHONE DATES TO APPOINTMENTS

To EMPHASIZE A KEY POINT, I WILL REPEAT MYSELF: Randomly dialing anyone is usually a fruitless endeavor. If you own a smartphone, you probably check to see who is calling before picking up. As salespeople, we pick up unknown callers more than the average American. That's because salespeople are prospectors, and it could be someone interested in what you do or sell.

The rest of the universe does not do this. Many years ago, I was a fan of "dialing sessions" (aka Phone Clinics) but I discourage them now. The current contact rate (a mere 9 percent) prevents advisors from successfully filling their calendars if they are only doing random dialing. It's time to get comfortable with another system.

Even in our personal lives, we quickly text a friend "*Talk?*" before calling. These are people who most likely pick up if you randomly dialed them. But more often than not, an unexpected call to a friend can result in an anxious-sounding "What's wrong?" at the other end.

In the financial world, some people have to be randomly dialed. Orphan clients—i.e., clients who do not have an assigned advisor to their account—are in this category. If we are unsure of a client's email address, we need to randomly dial. Calls to business phone numbers will more often get a pickup. Cold calling, by definition, is absolutely a random dialing activity.

In general, *you should request a convenient time to talk* before dialing clients, referrals, acquaintances, and prospects. This procedure creates two "appointments" in your calendar—one is the Phone Date (i.e., the agreed-upon time to talk on the phone to introduce the idea of the face-to-face event) and the other is the Appointment (the actual face-to-face event, in person or virtual). Use these two terms to keep these activities separate in your mind. But they both represent time saved on your calendar.

Scheduling a Phone Date

Setting Phone Dates is the best and easiest solution for a no-pick up culture. Very simply, you either text or email the prospect seeking a time that works for the two of you to speak briefly by phone. The content of this request is two sentences.

The first sentence is always unique to your relationship with that person. I will give examples, but you need to compose these for yourself. Remember, each relationship is different.

Example: You are referred to someone's sibling. Your client has sent your contact information to them, with a text asking them to accept your call (see chapter 14). Your first and second sentences to this new referral might be:

> **"I enjoyed my time with your sister, Reba, and I think you might want to edit some of the funny stories she's told me about the two of you. Send me some times you're available in the next two weeks for a brief phone call."**

Another example: You are reaching out to someone you know. Your children are friends, and this person is aware of the work that you do. You want to schedule a Phone Date, and, hopefully, a professional appointment. (You have to give some thought to these first sentences so the other person immediately knows it's from you.)

Your two sentences might be:

> **"I've enjoyed our conversations on the soccer bleachers and wanted to continue our discussion of your new business venture."**

The second sentence of a Phone Date request *must* be:

> **"Send me some times you're available in the next two weeks for a brief phone call."**

That's it. Don't change it. Don't make it a question either!

Of course, ideally, you would schedule an appointment when you're with the other parent in example 2, but sometimes that doesn't happen. (More on how to do that in chapter 8.)

More examples:

> **"It was great speaking to you at David and Julie's wedding. Your new business venture sounds exciting. Send me some times you're available in the next two weeks for a brief phone call."**

OR

> **"I know your brother has already introduced us by text. Send me some times you're available in the next two weeks for a brief phone call."**

The reason I harp on doing Phone Dates is because they frequently lead to appointments. Think about it—the other person already knows what you do and is agreeing to speak with you. If they are not interested in what you have to say, they won't respond to the Phone Date request. They'll ghost you. Getting a Phone Date brings you closer to the confirmed appointment.

I have to make one rule about Phone Dates clear: *Do not, I repeat, DO NOT text or email a request for a Phone Date to anyone you do not know.* An agency manager recently shared his group's phone-dates-to-appointments-statistics. They were abominably low—so low that I was concerned. A call with the entire management team established the problem right away—some of the advisors were emailing and texting Phone Date requests to *cold leads*. I don't know about you, but getting a text requesting that I call a stranger would only make me suspicious.

The managers were not clear that this activity is *only effective with people you know*—i.e., your natural market, people you've met at an event—*or referrals*. It works best with people who already have your contact information. Again, do not send out requests for Phone Dates to strangers.

I am always asked, "So how many Phone Dates do I need a week?" Agents want to know how many completed Phone Dates will get them their required appointments per week. The equivalent of "How many Phone Dates do I need?" used to be "How many dialing hours?" were required to schedule sufficient appointments. Let's do the numbers here.

Remember that my calculation are only for *first appointments*, either with a new person or an existing client. Most advisors would be happy to have 4 *new, confirmed appointments* per week. Here is my formula:

> To attain 4 confirmed appointments, you should be
> scheduling 6 unconfirmed.* We all know that some "in

---

* I get a lot of questions about that unconfirmed number. When people say they need to set more than 6 unconfirmed appointments to net the required 4, I hear that as a poor conversion from unconfirmed-to-confirmed appointments. That usually means one of two things. One, your script is not working well and the appointment the prospect agreed to is not clear to them. Or two, people are saying yes to just get you off the phone, because you are browbeating them.

pencil" appointments don't confirm for that week.

To have 6 unconfirmed appointments, you need 8 Phone Dates completed. Again, sometimes Phone Dates don't stick to the original date and time, so schedule 10 Phone Dates per week.

To have 10 "scheduled" Phone Dates per week you need to send out 12 requests for Phone Dates. If that doesn't work, send another dozen. (See Getting "Ghosted" below.)

Another caveat: If you are doing face-to-face marketing, you might be (should be) scheduling some appointments while having that in-person opportunity. Those appointments reduce your need to schedule 10 Phone Dates for that week. But sending out 12 Phone Date requests per week is a good habit to develop.

Getting "Ghosted"

Getting ghosted initially meant being ignored by someone you wanted to ask out on a date. It has now become part of our vernacular and we now refer to an ignored Phone Date request the same way. It's a different word for "ignored."

Let's suppose you send out a request for a Phone Date and nothing happens. A nonresponsive prospect makes us crazy, but it's helpful to not get distraught if your request is ignored. Remember, people have lives of their own; their lack of response is usually not directed at you specifically. Send another request in a couple of days. I usually wait at least four days, or even as much as a week most times.

If you continue to be ignored, move on. Find someone else. Do another marketing activity that brings more prospects into your life. You cannot keep pestering people.

A frequently posed question is how to be persistent without being a pest. The problem is that "being a pest" is in the eye of the beholder. Some people will admire you for reminding them that you want to speak to them, and others will get annoyed. If I knew the answer to which person was which, I'd tell you. Having a regular system will keep you from going nuts. I try once, wait four to seven days, and try again. If no response, I move on to other people and revisit this person a few weeks or months later. (See chapter 17.)

Know when to let it go, for now, but never give up on anyone. Put them on your newsletter list, holiday card list, or whatever system you have for communicating with clients and prospects. Keep the relationship going on your end. And try for an appointment at another time, and in a different way. For example, if you know you will see this prospect at an event, wait to speak to them in person.

The most important lesson is to not hang on to one prospect so avidly that you ignore your ongoing need to keep finding new people.

CHAPTER 6
COUNTING ACTIVITY

MOST MANAGERS COULD EASILY REPLACE the word "activity" with the word "appointments" and be more accurate. They routinely monitor advisors' calendars, and most companies have adopted a color-coded system. Different kinds of appointments have specific colors. This makes it easier to spot the appointments that represent meaningful conversations with new prospects versus time spent doing financial plans. I have had many conversations with managers who blithely say, "I expect all my advisors to have fifteen appointments per week." My question to that way of thinking: "How many of these are new, opening appointments with first-time clients?" And then the conversation usually gets more interesting.

The word "appointment" goes beyond an opening appointment with a new prospect. Other activities represent positive, career-building pursuits. For example, time with existing clients can represent "new activity" if the advisor is asking for referrals. Being at a networking event and creating a follow-up coffee appointment is the very definition of activity. Going to an event that has target-market opportunities is positive prospecting time. How does each manager calculate productive activity? Is everything an "appointment"?

There needs to be a better explanation of the word. I would propose that you count all appointments as activity *but classify them more distinctly.* Let's take the industry ideal of 15 appointments per week as an example.

A realistic expectation would be that 5 of these are new, "first" appointments; 5 are visits with clients that are now in the sales process (i.e., an initial appointment happened, the fact-find is completed, and there is a process that is moving along with mutual agreement); and 5 appointments represent marketing activities that will result in creating a first sales appointment.

First appointments are when you are sitting with a person or persons, who are ready, willing, and able to discuss their financial life. It can be a couple, an individual, or a business team fiscally responsible for a company. Anyone gets counted who is meeting with a financial advisor and understands that the agenda is their financial life. But if an advisor is conducting a "getting to know you" meeting and the prospect's finances are not being discussed, it's a marketing appointment. It counts, but it's different. (Think coffee and lunch appointments).

I often find that agencies are mushy in their definitions, which leads to a lot of ambiguous conversations between rookies and their managers. If everyone would clearly define the three types of appointments, then each manager can more easily see what their advisors are actually doing.

Again, the three types of appointments are:

First opening (or discovery) appointments

Marketing appointments (coffee appointments are the most common, but other activities count)

Sales Process appointments

Tons of people color coordinate their calendars. Instead of all "appointments" being one color, each of the above needs to be a different color so managers and advisors can quickly assess which is which.

Let's look at how this helps your weekly activity assessment: If you don't have enough fact-finding appointments, then the problem is that your marketing isn't creating prospects. Networking, in particular, can be unproductive if you go to a lot of meetings and don't "net" any clients from it. Being accurate in counting which activities need improvement is easier when you organize three separate but important skills into color-coordinated events.

Having a lot of "marketing" events on your calendar but without "opening" appointments generates a constructive conversation between an advisor and their manager. You need to focus on your marketing time and skills. Maybe you're not doing enough prospecting. Maybe you are going to events but not gaining relationships that convert to appointments.

If you have a lot of first appointments and not a lot of sales appointments, you are not creating the need with the first conversation in order to continue.

Some companies include personal time and "thinking" time. Those categories are also important. Now we need five different colors:

An opening appointment

A follow-up or closing appointment

A marketing activity

A personal time slot

A planning time

Creating a consistent, agency-wide system will help everyone keep track of what they are doing. If you have not been taught to do this, start such a system on your own. If whatever software you use doesn't allow color coordination, give each activity some kind of notation that allows you to readily see what your calendar looks like.

My calendar has colors for training events, phone calls, and flights. Assign a color to whichever activities are important for you to identify.

CHAPTER 7

YOU NEED TO MEET MORE PEOPLE

A DVISORS OFTEN CHALLENGE MY BELIEF that face-to-face marketing is critical for a successful financial career. The professionals in my workshops sometimes come from other industries and don't believe financial advisors need to get out and meet people. They cite numerous examples of why their previous careers were successful without those kinds of activities.

The problem with these comparisons is that financial services and the property and casualty industry require a high level of trust. There are numerous unique qualities to these industries, the most important of which is that *we are dealing with people's money.*

Most people require a high level of trust from three types of professionals. If you're going anywhere near my children, I need to trust you. If you are discussing anything about my personal health (both physical and mental), I need to trust you. And if you want to speak to me about my money, I need to trust you. This truth changes the playing field.

People try to do comparisons to other industries in myriad ways. But those comparisons fall flat. For a better career comparison, think of doctors. Rarely will someone new to a community choose a doctor from the internet. They will more likely ask neighbors for referrals. It's similar for financial advisors. However, the crucial difference between doctors and advisors is that doctors are often needed in unpleasant situations. I don't feel well, so I call the doctor. Rarely does someone "feel unwell" about their money. Our culture doesn't encourage going to a financial advisor regularly as much as it encourages going to dentists, doctors, and accountants.

Blame it on the marketing of the financial industry, but most Americans get their first paycheck without ever learning the basics of handling their money. The lack of financial training at a younger age brings adults to their first paying career with little understanding of managing their income.

The property and casualty sector has an advantage. You cannot go to the closing of your new house without providing proof of house insurance. Same thing for that shiny new car—call your insurance agent before the final papers are signed because you need to be covered. But how much do customers really understand their coverage? Not a lot.

Why am I harping on this phenomenon? Because it affects how financial advisors approach people. The phone is not ringing for most of the advisors I've met. The rare call to an advisor is often after some type of devastating financial blow. Sometimes, an older person will proactively refer a younger family member to their advisor. That's a blessing; if you are that lucky advisor, you've done a great job of letting your clients know that their children are never too young to start a relationship with a financial professional.

The cultural bias against this profession requires everyone to give pause before jumping on the "next new thing" in marketing. Social media is a great example of how some types of industries can thrive through specific marketing but others cannot. Many young people ask me why I'm not on Instagram. Probably because I teach something that is not visible—i.e., talking—and there is nothing to post that would be fun to look at. Advisors also ask me about Facebook. For every person who has done well having a business Facebook page, I know others who have been "unfriended" at the speed of light when they went too far on that platform. A professional FB page is fine, but don't mix up your business messages with photos of your pets.

LinkedIn has established itself as the "go to" website for businesses. I do not profess to be a LinkedIn specialist and will not advise you on how to properly message or write your bio. What I will tell you is how to conduct the first phone conversation if you've successfully messaged a connection. LinkedIn calls often don't have satisfying outcomes. You need to see them as networking conversations, not one-way dissertations on your practice. (See chapter 8.)

In general, your best bet for building and expanding your practice is to meet more people. In person. Shake people's hands, talk to them, look them in the eye as they speak to you, and be friendly.

I've told countless rookies that if you don't have an appointment scheduled for a weeknight, go to MeetUp.com and find an event to attend. Talk to people, talk to other people, and then talk to more people. Practice conducting conversations in which you ask people about themselves—and don't start with who you are. (And again, no elevator pitches, guys.) Never lose the opportunity to learn who other people are. Be an active listener.

My property and casualty agents do much less of this marketing than they should. It's the rare agent who has established himself or herself as *the* go-to person through strong community involvement. If you create the events that people want to go to, they will also want to do business with you. (More about this in chapter 9.)

I'm talking about more than just "networking." Being an active member of your community changes how people see you. It builds the very trust I am talking about. It is involvement, not just going to events and talking to a few people.

I have been active in my chamber of commerce since moving to Tennessee. If you ask me to refer you to a specific type of business-person, but I never used their services, I will still recommend a friend I know from my Chamber. Why? Because having spent time with that businessperson allows me to know their integrity, their personal style, and how reliable they are. *That* is why you get involved in your community. Not everyone needs to be using your services to have a high opinion of you as a businessperson.

Referrals make the world go around. Second to meeting someone in person, a referral from a client is the best way to build your practice. Many of us ask friends for referrals to movies, restaurants, different types of stores, websites, etc. Referrals will absolutely grow your practice. I do not teach you how to do that. (Go to *Resources*, page 135 for Bill Cates's contact info.) My job is to tell you how to get that person on the phone.

There are a lot of other marketing strategies that get you "names," but the ability to convert those names into appointments is key. I will be discussing most of them, but recognize that my preferences for specific marketing strategies are prejudiced by their ability to turn into an appointment. Doing other activities that don't *directly* create appointments are helpful, but know the difference between image building and appointment-setting activities.

Keep in mind that with so much scamming and dishonesty associated with the internet and the phone, there is a lot of defensiveness. Building a practice in a high-trust industry when people are so skeptical is challenging. Choose marketing activities that initiate a personal relationship and help build trust.

CHAPTER 8

NETWORKING CONVERSATIONS

A DVISORS NEED DIFFERENT TYPES OF TALKING SKILLS. The initial appointment is a very specific type of conversation, as is the closing appointment. Prior to any sales meeting, you need to create prospects—people who are interested in learning more about the work that you do. You need to have phone-talking skills as well. This profession requires you to be talented in different types of conversations. Two are on the phone and all the others are in person.

Here are three conversations that fall under the title of "networking:

> One: You are at an event, either business or social, and you want to engage with someone who is a possible prospect.

> Two: You make a phone call to someone with whom a "catch up" call is appropriate (think: friends and family you haven't seen for a long time).

> Three: You engage in successful messaging with someone on LinkedIn and are now set to speak on the phone for the first time.

All of these go under the heading of a "networking conversation." Most advisors and agents are not taught how to do this effectively. Or they're told to do the absolute wrong thing—i.e., share your business card and tell people what you do. Please don't.

Two major flaws mess up your networking. First, going into these conversations with the idea that you will absolutely set an appointment. That is the wrong mindset for this activity. Second, thinking "a friendly conversation" should create a follow-up professional appointment. That is also not true. I get a lot of calls from advisors who went to some kind of an event, met a "great person," and had a "terrific conversation." My questions about the event and conversation reveal that the two of them were golf fanatics and had a huge amount of fun yakking about their favorite sport. You cannot create a professional appointment from that type of conversation, but too many are doing this very thing. Yes, there is a ton of rapport and "liking" going on. But the conversation wasn't helpful to getting the other person to know who you are professionally. Being friendly is great; being *intentional* is better.

Important note about when you are networking: **Your conversations need to be *friendly* and *intentional*.**

Financial advisors and insurance agents are part of a highly misunderstood profession. If you are misunderstood, merely announcing what you do will not get you the outcome you want. You need to reverse your thinking. Every time you go to an event and meet people you don't know, keep one important sentence in your head:

You are there to find out who this other person is.

I work in an industry that embraces the concept of a "fact-find." A financial advisor doesn't make suggestions until they have asked their clients tons of questions about their money, their life, their hopes, and their dreams. There are two types of questions—factual ones (e.g., Where is your retirement plan? Do you have any life insurance at work? How much?) and emotional ones (How did your parents teach you about money as a child? What do you want your money to do for you and your children?). These questions help the advisor to understand the client's financial situation and assess their goals.

A networking conversation is similar. Your goal is to figure out who the other person is before you tell them who you are. This might conflict with information you have been taught in the past—i.e., use the dreaded, and dreadful, "Elevator Speech."

Let's take a detour here. An "Elevator Speech" implies a quick description of what you do. It should take you the same time to speak it aloud as a ride in an elevator—hence the nickname. Mostly it is two sentences. Sometimes it's just one. There *are* situations where you need an Elevator Speech. I've been to strict networking events where it goes around the room and you are told that when it comes to you, "Stand up and tell everyone what you do." Yes, you need your elevator pitch for *that* situation and *that* situation only.

The problem is when the Elevator Speech is used inappropriately. Like at certain networking and social events. Caveat: If you are going to a social event with absolutely no intention of creating professional relationships, use your Elevator Speech or a quick description of your work when you are asked what you do and you need to say it to keep the conversation going. Otherwise, don't.

Financial services requires you to be curious about others. If you aren't interested in who people are except mainly for their assets, then please put this book down. I will not be helpful to you. If you want to build a financial practice around people you like a lot and can help with their financial life, read on.

A good networking conversation actually has some easy rules you can follow. Here's a helpful sequence:

- Introduce yourself (even if you're wearing a name tag).

- Shake hands.

- Talk about the event you're at. ("Are you with the bride or groom?")

- Ask them about themselves. (Easiest: "What type of business are you in?")

- Start with neutral, non-threatening questions ("How long have you done this?" "When did your grandfather start this business?" "You're the fourth generation?" "Did you want to go into the family business?")

- Ask questions that get into more detail. (Go where *you* are most interested.)

- Keep track of details that you can refer to when it's your turn to talk.

- Always, always exchange information. (Remember your Digital Business Card.)

- Create another meeting, someplace else for another time (aka an appointment).

Let me expand on each of these steps. Start by talking about what you and the other person share—the event (obviously) or the weather. Yes, this is why we all talk about the weather! No matter where we are, all of us are subjected to it. Everyone likes to complain about weather and delight in it when it's good. It's an ice breaker, folks! Don't be afraid to go there.

Your event is the main thing you're sharing with this stranger. "Do you come here often?" can be a pickup line, or an ice breaker at a recurring business meeting. More importantly, ask the other person if they come often because they are gaining something from the meetings. That can lead you to other questions you want to ask.

At networking events you must find out who the other person is looking to meet (for their business purposes). Two reasons for this.

One, you get to know whom you can refer them to since networking isn't just about you. And two, you need to know this information so you have your Get Out of Jail Free Card.

Here are your first four questions:

Have you been to this event before?

What keeps you coming back? (Or why did you pick this one?)

Are there other events you attend?

Whom are you looking to meet here?

Continue asking them about their business by going from general (nonthreatening) questions to more specific. However, if you are unable to relate to this person and not "connecting," your fourth question will help you to exit the conversation gracefully. But do not plan your exit until a full three to four minutes have passed. Here's a story to explain:

A few years ago, I found myself with an inexperienced networker at a Chamber meeting. He was a painter and no matter what I asked him, I got one- or two-word answers. I knew quickly that I was not going to be helpful to him, so I wanted to exit the conversation gracefully. Luckily, I knew how to do this because I used the above four questions at the beginning, I knew he was looking for corporations or homeowners who needed a paint job in the very near future. So I used the following gracious exit line:

"Peter, you've told me who you're looking to meet. I'm not that person, so I'm going to let you go in order to find that person. If I meet someone who fits the profile, I will make sure to walk them over to you and make an introduction."

In such a circumstance, you then shake their hand and move on to the next person.

This works well. It's also socially gracious and effective. Do not suddenly say, "I have to go speak to someone who just walked in." It always makes the person you're speaking to feel unimportant. And it's rude.

Back to the beginning: You have introduced yourself, chatted about the event, and then asked the other person what they do. In America, this is perfectly acceptable social conversation. We talk about work in this country. And people happily talk about their work if you keep asking them questions. And that's the key! Keep asking questions and make sure your questions get you the critical information you want to know.

Quick side note: What do you do if the other person asks you about your profession before you get a chance to ask them? Good question. I am going to give you an answer you probably won't like, but do it anyway. Say to them: *"I'm boring. Let's talk about you"* and immediately follow it with more questions. If that suggestion is too short, you can say, *"I'm a consultant and I'm boring. Let's talk about you."* It works. Every advisor who has used this technique told me that the other person never remembers you said you were boring. What they always remember is that you asked them a lot of questions and listened intently.

This is where most networking problems reside. Many advisors are good at being super friendly and engaged but their conversations are not purposeful. You want to be the best questioner on the planet and ask the other person strategic questions about their life—whether it's personal or business oriented. Too many advisors ask questions but don't know what they are listening for. *You are listening for aspects of their life in which the work that you do can be meaningful and helpful to them.*

At *no point* do you jump in and say, "I can help you with that" when you uncover problem areas. Just keep listening. You are definitely looking for the issues that relate to your work, but you have to learn to listen and "keep mental notes" about the parts of their narrative that pique your interest.

Let's say you successfully engage someone at a networking event around the business they own. You're asking great questions about their employees, how they survived various recessions and the pandemic, who their key people are, etc. While asking questions, you need to keep track of which part of the conversation will help you to create your "transition" statement when it's your turn to talk.

Does this person have effective benefits? Do they find they have a lot of turnover? Do they lose their executives? Are they unsure how to exit their business because they never valued and sold one? Are they afraid to leave their executive job because they don't know if they actually have enough to retire on? If you need to know about these things, direct the conversation to these topics *through your questions.* Don't let tangents drift both of you away from the part of their life that interests you.

You can get more specific, and personal, if the conversation goes on for more than 10 minutes. Fifteen is better. If you don't know how to engage someone in a conversation about their work life for 15 minutes, you need to learn how. I have a list of questions for both business and social networking events to help you. (See page 105.)

While you are doing the questioning, you need to start composing your words for when it's your turn to talk. How does that happen? If you're questioning another human being for more than 15 minutes, they will get "on a roll" and keep answering you and giving you information. At the point at which you want to turn the tables, **take a pregnant pause.** Two ways to do this: If you're at an event with a meal, go back to your food. Cut your meat. Butter a piece of bread. If you're standing at an outdoor event, sip your drink. Once the other person hears the silence, it will occur to them that they have been doing all the talking. They will never realize it was your constant questioning that provoked it. All they know is that you're interested in them. Polite conversation rules say it's now their turn to ask you, "So what do *you* do?"

You need to believe me that this works. The pregnant pause is magic.

I've done this dozens of times and every time I create a short silence, the other person says, *"So what do you do?"* I usually can't repress a smile. It's like clockwork. Now you have an interested person asking you about your work.

DO NOT GIVE YOUR ELEVATOR SPEECH AT THIS MOMENT.

If you do, you will blow it. Instead, start your next sentence with, "***You know, when you said . . . ?***" and you need to fill in the sentence with (verbatim) something they said which relates to your work.

Here are examples:

> "*You know when you said* that your little tech company loses your best employees to the Big Guys? I have another tech client who is in the same situation."

> "*You know when you said* you have no idea if you have enough money to walk away from your business? Several of my clients were in that exact situation."

> "*You know when you said* you and your wife have no idea how to save for your own retirement and send your three children to college? Several of my clients are in your shoes."

You relate to *their* problems by letting them know that you deal with those challenges all the time. None of these answers should be "I'm a financial advisor at ABC Company." No one cares *where* you work. They care that you can do something to improve their lives. *Every conversation will require a unique answer when you get asked what you do.*

That is what networking sounds like.

Let's relate this technique to two types of phone calls. One, for people in your natural market you haven't seen for over a year. Two, LinkedIn connections who are willing to have a "get to know you" phone call. The same rules apply. You use your questioning skills to first find out what is going on with the other person and *then* you tell them how your work fits into their picture. Notice how the transitioning sentence is written? "*You know when you said . . .* " does not have the word "I" in it.

Most of the time your transition statements will pique the other person's interest because *you are still talking about them.* The next potential hazard is when they ask you, "How did you do that?" *or* "How did you help them?"

Now you're in a danger zone.

This is when many advisors make a huge mistake. Either they give too much information, fall into "education mode," or talk about the solution they provided to the client that shares the problem. All of those are incorrect. Look at it this way: You now have an interested party. Suggest another meeting. Here is the better answer to "How did you do that for your client?"

> **"I think we should continue our conversation in a more private place. Let's have coffee next week."**

OR

> **"I'd love to give you the details around how I solved that for my other business owners. Let's go to lunch next week and I can share more with you."**

And pull out your calendar!!

On the phone, your major adjustment is the lack of the visual, so your pregnant pause will be a long drink of water, thereby creating silence. Expect the other person to say, "*So what do you do?*" and be prepared with your *"You know when you said . . . ?"* statement.

This works. I do it all the time. The only time I use an Elevator Speech is when I want to shut down a conversation (like on a plane when I want to read my book since I've been teaching all day). My favorite is *"I'm a telemarketing trainer."* No one bothers me after that.

If you want to "practice" your networking conversations, go to MeetUp.com and pick an event to go to. If you're not a natural talker, my suggestions are a bit challenging at first. But keep practicing. You need to learn to have "no goal" conversations. Go to Starbucks and talk to people. Practice on people you see regularly but have never asked about themselves—like your favorite vendors. Even while practicing, you will be stunned at how much people like to talk about themselves when there is a good listener encouraging them. Be that listener.

You have one goal—learning to engage others through questions. The better you get at asking people about themselves, the more often you will walk away with a follow-up appointment.

OR—think of it as fact-finding, but it's about who people are, not their finances!

(For more information on being a good networker, reach out to my friend and colleague Michael Goldberg, whose contact information is on page 135.)

CHAPTER 9

FACE-TO-FACE MARKETING IDEAS

I've STATED MANY REASONS TO INCLUDE face-to-face activities in your week. More people will want to work with you if they feel they know you. The only type of lead that is comparable is a referral. More on those later.

Each of the ideas I've shared has been effective for some advisors. Not all of them will work for you, but a marketing idea will never work if you don't give it. Creating a target market for your practice will increase the effectiveness of networking because you will start to "become known" in a circle of people who matter to you. Choosing and committing to a target market have made a lot of advisors very successful. In advance of spending money and time, you also need to figure out which target market is viable for you.

A target market is not the same as a demographic group. Don't confuse them. A target market is a group of people who have something in common and have a means of communicating among themselves. Statistically speaking, common sets of people are *not* a target market—e.g., people over fifty-five who have assets in excess of $105,000. That's a demographic.

Professional groups that have a local organization which meets regularly are a target market. When I moved from New York to Tennessee, my first inquiry was to the local NAIFA chapter because I wanted to find my local financial buddies. If you are targeting lawyers, find the local bar association.

Here is a list of marketing ideas I've shared with or gotten from many advisors. Not all will be helpful to you, but when you pick one, implement it consistently:

> **Small breakfasts:** Instead of planning an expensive and complicated seminar, invite four of your favorite clients who share something in common to breakfast. Look through your client files. You probably will find a trend of clients who share the same profession. Let's say your targeted group is architects. You invite four architect clients to a "special" breakfast meeting and ask them to bring another architect friend as their guest. You are *not* the speaker. Invite a center of influence (COI) professional who has something of interest to say to this group. I recommend you select a nice hotel that serves a buffet breakfast. You are now paying for ten breakfasts—yourself, the speaker/COI, four clients and four guests. Your speaker limits their talk to twenty minutes. The rest of the time is spent networking and getting to know each other. Do this once a month and you can clone your favorite clients in an inexpensive, fun way. *Plus* your COI is now in your debt. (Make sure your chosen speaker is actually an engaging and interesting one. They are a reflection on you since you're introducing four favorite clients to them.)
>
> **Community groups (political, civic, volunteer):** Join groups that represent something of genuine interest to you. You can't volunteer with the ulterior motive of "creating" clients. Everyone can detect a "wolf in the hen house," which defeats

your purpose. Be generous and volunteer with sincerity, and your relationships will develop over time. Pick something you're interested in and you'll also have fun.

Trade shows/fairs/expos: Carefully choose the events you participate in. Having a booth is an expense that will not work for you if you don't have the right people coming to the event. Make sure to keep your booth visibly "open" and not blocked by the table provided. Put the table perpendicular to the traffic flow so you can stand close to people as they walk by. Your goal is conversations with people, not just handing out brochures they won't read. (See chapter 8 on Networking.)

Planned events (client in-house events): Most advisors and agents like hosting events. For my P&C agents, you want to be the "go-to" place for every holiday. Clients with young children need ideas for what to do with their little ones. Be that place! Have an event at your location or the local park for each major holiday. This will do a lot to create good feelings about your agency. For my financial advisors and managers, I become "the" educational agency in your community. Social Security seminars given by credentialed people are a big draw for a specific age group. Younger families need to learn how to save for college, which is a hot issue right now. Make sure no one leaves without having your contact in their phones so your follow-up is productive.

Hobbies: Many advisors are timid about talking to the friends they play with. The most common reason is "I don't want to be pushed out of my favorite tennis group" or golf foursome. I understand that but it might not be a valid concern. Remember, these are people you like; in your professional capacity you might have important knowledge that could benefit them. The challenge is usually what to say to them, which is addressed in chapter 13, but you should at least feel an obligation to offer them time with you.

Networking: Choose your events carefully. You can't create relationships in just one meeting. Go to two or three events before you make up your mind to join a group with a fee. I've been to events where the atmosphere "felt right" and there were others I tried three times and couldn't click with anyone. Remember, if a group doesn't meet often enough, you won't be able to build relationships. A minimum of once a month is best.

Seminars: Agency managers are increasingly sponsoring seminars for specific populations. The speaker and subject are selected by the managers; the advisors are asked to invite their clients, friends, and family. The biggest challenge is the advisor invitation phone calls. Managers complain to me that the events are poorly attended, including people who said they would come but don't. That speaks to the invitation phone call (see page 100). If you are asked to invite people to an agency-sponsored seminar, make sure to make your calls promptly and send out follow-up reminders the day before and/or of the seminar.

Canvassing: My rendition of canvassing is different from what was done generations ago. Instead of plotting out a map of places to walk to business owners, use your current appointments to meet the neighbors of your existing clients. Most financial cases require several meetings. Ask your client who their next-door neighbor is—whether it's a suite next door or in a strip mall. Get their permission to share that they are your client. Then when you visit your client, include time for visits to the other business owners nearby. Oftentimes, clients will give you great "intel" on their neighbors. They usually know who just moved in, who is thinking of retiring and/or selling, etc. Adding these short hello visits to your calendar will create new prospects.

Everyday situations: Sometimes you're standing in line and talking to someone who is interesting. Learn to move quickly into your networking conversation mode. I did this on a slow "trainee line" at the supermarket. A few years ago, in our mutual frustration, the woman ahead of me at checkout turned around and rolled her eyes at the slowness of our line. I laughed but also noticed and admired her necklace. A few questions later I find out she was an artist who created unique pieces. After about five more minutes, I was referring her to my jeweler who loves distinctive pieces for her shop. It can happen just like that.

Social Situations (parties, events): I clearly stated in chapter 8 that you might have an opportunity to turn a social situation into a professional one. If you just want to have a good time at an event, don't feel the need to pursue a networking conversation. Just have fun. But if you find out that you are seated next to the CEO of a Fortune 100 company, you might change how you engage that person. Remember, asking questions is the key.

Natural Market: We will talk about how to call your friends and family in chapter 13.

CHAPTER 10

VIRTUAL APPOINTMENTS

THE PANDEMIC HAS CHANGED OUR LIVES in myriad ways. Professionally, we were able to adapt because virtual software gave us the opportunity to conduct visual meetings. Although it seemed like a "stop gap" at the time, we continue to see the advantages of this technology. Virtual appointments are here to stay.

Initially, virtual appointments were not confirming at the same rate as in-person appointments. They require the addition of new habits to your appointment-setting phone call. You also need to establish your client's comfort with the virtual format before you get off the phone. Remember, this industry is very tech-savvy. Many potential clients are not used to the software that is second nature to us. Be sure to ask if they are familiar with the software your company uses. Don't assume they know what to do with the link you've sent them or that they understand all the little icons and emojis we love so well. Here is how to ensure your virtual appointments stick:

1. The changes in the phone call are simple. At the end of your script, use a new alternative choice close. You don't always have to stick to time ("Which is better for you, earlier or later in the week?") or place ("We can either meet at your office or mine.")

47

It can now be the format of your appointment. Example:

"Some of my clients are comfortable with an in-person appointment, but we also have the option for a virtual one. Which do you prefer?"

OR

"I've been meeting many of my clients through Zoom, but I am also happy to meet you in person at my office, or yours. Which option is best for you?"

2. When sending an appointment reminder email the day before your appointment, resend the link and add instructions on how to use the software.

Here is verbiage for the reminder: *"Looking forward to seeing you on our appointment tomorrow morning. Here is the link again."*

Attach instructions to your confirmation email on how to get onto the meeting,(e.g., "click the link"), what the icons are used for, and how to mute and unmute. Too much of a prospect's patience can get wasted on just getting into the meeting—which is an awkward way to start the appointment. Other people will be comfortable with virtual software, but not necessarily the software your company uses.

Clarify all of this before you end the call! I know it sounds tedious, but so is having the prospect unable to log on to your meeting. Perhaps they are getting frustrated with the technology.

Some advisors resend the link five to ten minutes before their meeting. You never know how many other emails your client received since the initial phone call. Sometimes it's just buried, and the client, unable to find it, just skips the appointment. Don't let that happen.

CHAPTER 11

UNDERSTANDING SCRIPTS & RESPONSES

M Y TRAINING FOCUSES ON TWO APPOINTMENTS: an initial appointment for both financial advisors and property and casualty agents, and then regularly scheduled appointments with clients for my P&C agents. In either case, the way a script is written is the same. It is only the specific wording that changes.

When you call someone who is expecting the call, i.e., you scheduled a Phone Date, you need to be efficient and respectful of their time. You also need to be friendly, so I will directly address the challenge of "How are you?"

The first part of the call is what you say, which we will call your script. The second part is handling their response (see page 56).

There are seven components to an effective appointment-setting script:

A—Greeting
B—Introduction
C—Your company (sometimes)
D—The Connector
E—Your offering
F—The benefit
G—The close

The structure never changes, just the words you choose. Let's go through each part with an explanation and examples:

A: Always open a call with a greeting. Avoid slang. During role plays, in an effort to sound friendly, many advisors resort to "hey" or greetings that are too casual. You will sound more professional if you just say, *"Hello, "Good morning/afternoon/evening,"* or *"Hi."*

B: Then introduce yourself if they don't know you. You can skip this if you are in the prospect's phone as a Contact and have a scheduled Phone Date. Expect those people to say, "Hi, (Your Name)" when they pick up because they know it's you. If that happens, just say, *"Hi"* back.

We need to take an important detour here. Most people automatically add "How are you? "at this point in the call. **Do not do that.** With friends and family, it's too easy to get caught up in a long conversation about whatever they want to talk about. Remember, if the other person doesn't know this is a professional call, you might end up going off on a huge tangent and lose the other person to call waiting. In order to keep all of this under control, say hello, then immediately follow with a critical sentence:

"Hi, it's Gail and I'm calling for two reasons." This is one of my favorite sentences. When you say you are calling for two reasons, the other person knows you have more than one thing to talk about. When you *do* ask about their life, they tend to keep their answer shorter. This is the magic of words. You can politely reduce the "how are you" chitchat. Here is how you do it.

Start with, "The first reason for my call . . . " and then follow it with a **one-topic** question. (That's the problem with "How are you?" It's open-ended and vague, thereby inviting topics you don't want to get into.) When you ask, *"How is John enjoying his first year at college?"* you are being specific, and so will your prospect. Again, the opening of a phone call is, *"Hi, (their name), I'm calling for two reasons. Did the roofer come and fix the problem you were having?"*

It stuns my advisors when they can actually move on to their agenda after using this technique. You're being thoughtful, and yet you get the other person to reduce their answer to your question. *They know there is something else on the agenda.* That is why this statement "I'm calling for two reasons" has to become a habit.

After you talk for a couple of minutes about their personal life, transition to *"The other reason for my call . . . "* and into the rest of your script.

You MUST practice and memorize this. Your old habits will kick in if you don't work at changing your opening line. Please write it down and put it in front of where you make your calls:

"Hi, _____, it's (your name) and I'm calling for two reasons."

An important part of this substitute for *"How are you?"* is that you have to know the person well enough to compose a question about their life. If you cannot compose a highly specific question, you can't use this technique. I think that "How are you?" to people you don't know is disingenuous. I work with many advisors who specialize in the education arena and they call on many teachers. When we role play and they say, *"Hello, Mrs. Smith, this is John with ABC Company. How are you doing today?"* It makes me cringe. The *"How are you?"* is not sincere, it's knee-jerk. I think we need to be more strategic in the hello portion of a call and not knee-jerk any version of *"How are you?"*

For those people you can ask something specific, allow a minute or two for the question to be answered. Don't rush.

Another alternative for *"How are you?"* is *"Hi, it's Gail Goodman, and I know you're busy so I'll be brief."* And keep talking. Your script is not that long if it's done right. The suggested format, from A to G, creates scripts that are less than a minute. Other than the opening personal question, the rest of the script should not exceed forty-five seconds.

C: Your company name is most important when calling Company-Provided leads. (See chapter 16.) In most other cases, you don't have to state your company name because that is included in your Digital Business Card. Any marketing program that is initiated by your company or agency requires you to add the company name when you say "Hello" because it's part of your identity to that person.

Most often, you will not say your company name. (For my P&C friends, the team members and staff are trained to always say the company name, even to customers, so keep doing that.)

D: Now we are at the critical part of your script. The D is "the Connector," and here is where you tell the prospect why you are on their phone. Don't say this: *"I'm calling to schedule an appointment."* No, you're not. The appointment is the *outcome* of the call, not the *reason* for it. This distinction is tricky.

Naming this portion "the Connector" makes it easier to write. Think of how you know this person. If you are referred, you will mention the referring person's name. If you met at an event, you will mention the event. If it's your grandmother, you need to tell her you are calling in your professional capacity.

The D part of a script needs to be written differently for different groups of people. I've separated your leads into three different groups to help write this portion:

D1: Memory Jog leads. Anyone who knows you or has met you falls into this category—e.g., friends and family, people with whom you share hobbies, vendors you use, alumni groups you belong to, former co-workers or clients, current clients, seminar attendees, people you meet at expos/fairs/shows, canvassed leads, your neighbors, people you meet at social or networking events, charities, political groups, civic or volunteer groups in which you're active, people you meet accidentally while doing what you do around your community, all the folks you know through your children's activities, etc. In essence, anyone who has met you in person and knows who you are.

D2: This group is comprised of people you've **been told to call by someone else**. The best type of D2 lead is an introduction—aka a referral. The other people you are "told to call" could be leads provided by your company (orphan policy holders;,calling another agent's "neglected" clients, associations for which you/your company provides their benefits). Lastly, some young advisors are partnered with older ones and asked to call their C+D clients.

D3: These leads are the hardest because you have no relationship with them. The four major types of leads in this group are **direct mail/email responders; purchased leads** (from a company that sells them to you because those prospects are interested in a specific product or idea); **internet leads** (when you sign up to receive requests for quotes on products via various internet sites); and, finally, **cold calls**. There aren't any cold lead scripts in this book because my goal is to eliminate the need for this type of prospecting in your practice. But there *are* many of you who get internet leads for specific products, such as health insurance and both car and home insurance. (See chapter 15.)

E: The E statement is when you mention the idea of getting together but you are not at the point of asking for the appointment. The E statement is made up of three parts:

Invitational verb + Action verb + Noun

An invitational verb invites the prospect to be with you. Some good verb phrases would be "get together," "meet," "schedule an appointment," "have coffee," or "get on the calendar."

The action verb is what you do when you get together. Words like "discuss," "share," "talk about," and "provide" fall into this section. Lastly, you end the sentence with a noun.

Here are examples of E sentences:

> *"I'd like to get together to share with you the total scope of the work that I do."*

"I want to <u>schedule</u> a time when we can <u>sit and talk</u> about <u>your concerns</u> regarding your retirement plan."

"I'd like to <u>meet for coffee</u> so we can <u>continue our conversation</u> from the <u>meeting</u>."

"I'd like to <u>visit</u> and <u>share</u> with you the <u>ideas</u> that your sister thought were important."

F: This is the most forgotten part of any appointment-setting script. It is the benefit of the appointment for the prospect. Not the benefit of any specific product but just having an initial appointment with you. Most advisors agree that an initial appointment provides good information to the prospect on the breadth of your work. Again, being in a misunderstood professional requires you to share the vast scope of what you and your company provide. The tricky part of writing a benefit is that you have to remember it is the *positive emotional outcome of the appointment for the prospect.* You are not selling a product, but rather you are proposing a new relationship to this person.

So the benefit (F Statement) might be as an example:

"That way, you can use me, my company, and all the resources we have in any way that makes you feel the most comfortable."

G: Here is where you ask for the appointment. Use an alternative choice close. If you can provide the meeting through virtual software, you can use that as a new close.

Here are some ideas for various closes:

"I have been meeting in person with some of my clients, but other people prefer to do it virtually. Which is easier for you?"

"I am happy to visit with you either virtually or in person. Which is better?"

"What is the least hectic time in your day—before or after lunch?"

"What is the easiest time in your work week—the earlier or later part?"

Do not ask yes or no questions at the end. Closes such as "Does that sound interesting to you?" are deadly!

Here's an interesting psychological fact: Most people, when offered two choices, will pick the second choice more than 50 percent of the time. Note the order in which I did the "when we meet" close. That is also the reason I don't like to use "days or evenings." It's better to say, *"Which is easier for you—earlier or later in the day?"* Keep the second choice as your favorite.

When you put all of these components together, it looks like the script below. I call this my "Apology Tour Script," and it is specifically for experienced advisors who have not called their friends and family. Since you know them, I did not include the company name. I have added the letters that represent each part of the script format.

"Hi, this is Gail, and I'm calling for two reasons. (A & B) How are you handling Jessica being away at college? (Let this part go for a minute or two.)

"The other reason for my call is that you know that I've been in financial services for over ten years, and in all that time I've never called you on a professional basis. I'd like to rectify that with this phone call and position myself as an additional financial resource to you and your family. (D) We can set a time for me to visit with you and Bob, and I can show you the total scope of the work that I do. (E) That way, you can use me, my team, and all the resources I have at my

disposal in any way that makes you feel the most comfortable. (F) I know that even with your youngest away at college, you are still very busy, so what is the least hectic time for you generally—earlier or later in the week? (G)"

Response Handling

There are only four categories of response when you offer an appointment. Despite rumor to the contrary, everything that isn't a yes is not an objection. Try to get that thought out of your head.

Here are the four categories of response:

1. They agree to the appointment.

If you do an alternative choice close and they pick one, you've got an appointment. "Which is easier for you—earlier or later in the week?" "Earlier is better." Now you need to narrow down the details. Once you hear this type of a "yes," start offering to them an appointment time that is convenient for your calendar. If you offer a virtual or in-person appointment and they say, "Let's do virtual" go back to the chapter on Virtual Meetings and follow my recommendations. Virtual meetings are great once they happen but are often stymied by the prospect's lack of technological expertise. Without being condescending, make sure they understand how to use your company's preferred software. I suggest that all my advisors and managers create a simple "How to get on to (Zoom)" list of steps to send to a client who isn't confident around the software you use.

2. They either say "I'm not interested" or "I'm all set."

This is a very small category because it only represents these specific sentences. These two sentences have stumped most phoners ever since the very early days of telemarketing in America. They are knee-jerk responses to the script and require you to dig a little deeper so you get a more specific answer.

In response to *"I'm not interested,"* ask in a polite tone of voice,

"May I ask why not?" If they repeat, *"Because I'm just not interested,"* let it go and get off the phone. The goal of the question is to get more specifics. If you hear *"Because I have an advisor"* or *"Because I don't have enough money and will waste your time"* or a million other things, that's good. You're getting a more complete answer which takes you out of this category. You're now handling a Category 4 response. I'll get to that soon. For "I'm all set," just ask, "What exactly do you mean?"

3. They ask you a question.

This is easy if you can contain yourself. Simply answer them as briefly as possible and then ask for the appointment again. Questions tend to get us excited because they show interest. Here are the most common ones you'll hear:

"How long is this going to take?" "Usually we spend about 20-30 minutes on the first meeting. What time is easier for you—earlier or later in the day?"

"What is this going to cost?" "There is no fee for our initial meeting. Would it be easier to do this virtually or at your office?"

"Does my spouse need to be there?" "Usually it's better if both of you are there since most of the time, questions from wives and husbands tend to be different. When is the best time to meet with both of you—during the week or on the weekend?"

4. The client states a problem.

I hate the word "objection" because it is a misnomer. The prospect is not objecting to anything. They're telling you a problem. There is a reality that exists for them that gets in the way of scheduling the appointment. Most common of all is when they say, *"I already have an advisor."* Your ability to smoothly answer this one is critical. I like to utilize a modern version of the feel-felt-found technique because it does important things. First, it acknowledges that you heard what the person said. Second, it tells the prospect they are not alone and you've heard this before. And lastly, it offers them a short story about how other people—who had that exact problem—took a leap of faith and met with you and got a benefit from that meeting. You need to take the time to memorize good answers to the most common problems you will hear. Hands down, "I have an advisor" wins this contest every time. Make sure you can answer it smoothly.

Here are my favorite answers to some common problems:

"I have an advisor."

"I hear you, and most of the people I call already work with some kind of financial professional. But I will make you two promises as the basis for this meeting. One, I will never undo any good work another professional has done for you. And two, any ideas I DO suggest will only be those that complement your existing portfolio. With that as the premise for a cup of coffee, which is easier for you, earlier or later in the day?"

"I don't have enough money to have an advisor."

"I hear you and, unfortunately, other people have said the same thing. But after meeting with me they found that the work that I do is about organizing your money and not necessarily spending more. What is less hectic for you—this week or next?"

"I'm really busy now."

"I understand, and most people are very busy. But they also found, after meeting with me, that part of my role is to take the burden of thinking about your money off your shoulders and put it on mine. For busy people, they are relieved to know I'm doing that for them." (Ask for the appointment.)

"Email me something."

"I hear you and some of my clients initially think that an email will be sufficient. But they found, after meeting with me, that because the information on websites is usually generic, but their financial lives are specific, that a face-to-face meeting is far more beneficial." (Ask for the appointment.)

"The market is too volatile."

"I understand what you're saying, and other clients thought that now was not a good time to meet due to the market fluctuations. But they found, after talking with me, that it was comforting to speak to a financial professional to make sure they're doing all they can in this market, and I'd like to do that for you as well." (Ask for the appointment.)

"I have a family member who takes care of this."

"I hear you and I have met other people who initially worked with someone in their family. But they found, after a visit with me, that, in fact, they were more comfortable speaking about their finances with me because I WASN'T a family member. You may find that to be true as well." (Ask for the appointment.)

Holidays

Let's face it. For the past few years, holiday season starts right after Halloween. This phenomenon puts a strain on everyone when stores start hanging red and green Christmas décor right after taking down the pumpkins. Your clients and prospects might feel more pressure starting early November because of this cultural shift. Many advisors just give up prospecting once we reach Thanksgiving, but don't do that. You have a lot of reasons to meet with new people late in the year as much as you do at any other time of year. The challenge is in having a succinct, intelligent response to them when they say, "Call me in the new year" or some version of it. Here are some classic statements you will hear during holiday time, and how to handle them:

"I'm too stressed out by the holidays to focus on this."

"I hear you, and most of my clients are pretty stressed out at this time of year, but they found, after meeting with me ,that a coffee appointment (or lunch) was the one break they could look forward to in the middle of the chaos. I'd like to do that for you. Where should we meet—at Starbucks or Dunkin' Donuts?" (Or name two restaurants.)

"My family is about to descend on me and I've got too much to do."

"I understand, and many of my clients are in that exact situation. But they found, after meeting with me, they were glad that they did. This is a time to be thinking about family and our conversation was, in fact, about providing for your family. I think you'll find that having our appointment now makes a lot of sense. When should we get together—earlier or later this week?"

"My business is really crazy this time of year. Call me in January."

"I hear you, and most of my business clients are finding this time of year very stressful and busy. But they found, after meeting with me, that some of the ideas that we may discuss could be calendar sensitive and to discuss them would be timely. I think it's important enough to schedule before the end of the year. What's easier for you—this week or next?"

Beware of Over-Scripting.

Let's say you've already met someone, spoken to them in person (such as at a social or business event), and now you're making a follow-up call. You scheduled a Phone Date, which confirmed, and they pick up when you dial them. Do not use a full A-B-C-D-E-F-G script—it won't be required. If you have advanced the relationship in person, and the phone call is only to nail down a specific date and time for an appointment, don't overtalk. You might only need to say:

> *"Hi, it's Gail, and I really enjoyed our conversation at Richard's party last week. We talked about getting together to discuss more about your business. I have my calendar open, so tell me which is better for you—later this week or should we look at next week?"*

Using a full A-B-C-D-E-F-G script would be inappropriate and too wordy.

CHAPTER 12
FIVE PHONE MISTAKES & DIRTY WORDS

THERE ARE FIVE CRITICAL PHONE ERRORS THAT MANY ADVISORS unwittingly make. Knowing what these errors are will help you avoid them. However, habits are hard to break, so use visual clues to help yourself stick to your script.

1. **Assumptive language:** You might be saying words that sound as if you are already the prospect's advisor. My training focuses on the *first* appointment, which is where you are interviewing for the job of being their advisor. The biggest word mistake here is the use of the word "help" followed by the word "you." That combination—"help you" —puts you in the position of already being their advisor, so it is critical to *not* say those words together. The word "help" on its own can work for you. Example: *"My practice focuses on helping small business owners to keep more of their money and give less to Uncle Sam."* Here you are using the word "help" in a neutral, group context. Once you add "you," it is like pointing a finger at the prospect and it sounds assumptive.

2.   **Ad-libbing:** Take my word for this: You don't sound more natural when you ad-lib on the phone. You sound like you're grasping for words and often end up babbling. Sounding "scripted" can be corrected, but ad-libbing is worse. To sound more natural with a script, write the key phrases in a list and use that document to prompt yourself when on the call. You will stick to the good language you chose. You will talk more naturally. Once you start ad-libbing, you can get into trouble because of the next problem.

3.   **Using Sales Language** on the phone instead of Phone Language. All salespeople need to be bilingual. You need one language for setting your appointments and a different set of words for doing your sales call. They are not the same! One major mistake on the phone is "menu-ing" the list of products you offer. That is not helpful because of Mistake No. 1—you're not their advisor. You cannot sell the products without first selling yourself. You have to create a relationship with the prospect before they consider any products. Last I heard, you are also supposed to conduct a financial conversation to find out what is important to each client. So listing products is not helpful. It represents a classic way your Sales Language can easily overtake your Phone Language when the latter is weaker. You need to have a large repertoire of phone words in order to stick to the right language when you're scheduling the first appointment.

4.   **Being "too relaxed"** sounds ridiculous, but financial advisors have to avoid sounding blasé. You need to be friendly and professional, but sometimes the friendly part deteriorates into being too lax. The very beginning of a script—i.e., the Hello—sets the tone for your call. Using slang or saying, "Hey" instead of "Hello" immediately reduces your professionalism. Remember, on the phone your words and inflection are the only tools you have, so give them the respect they deserve. You don't need to

sound overly serious or dour, but you do need to be professional.

5. **Forgetting the benefit statement** (the F) is the most common error. Even when an advisor *has their script in front of them*, with a benefit statement written, it is easy to just swing from the E (I'd like to schedule a time where I can show you the total scope of the work that I do) into the close. The benefit statement tells the client why the appointment is good for them. The E statement may sound great, but there needs to be one more sentence, and that's the one that is most forgotten. Make a point of writing the benefit statement in large bold type someplace you can easily see when calling to remind yourself to say it out loud. When you forget the F statement, the prospect is thinking "What's in this for me?"

Dirty Words

I have given out my list of **Phone Dirty Words** for decades. These words are related to my concern you are using *Sales* Language on the phone, and not *good* Phone Language. There are many words that work perfectly well in person but have a different flavor when used on a phone call. The full list will be at the end, but some of the most common, and most egregious, words need further explanation.

Review: I get a lot of pushback from agents about removing this word from their language. The reason it has to go is because it doesn't work! Americans don't want to review anything—their insurance for sure. You need to use *more words* to defend the idea of the appointment. You're better off saying what the review process is, instead of shortcutting it with a single (ineffective) word. Your process is important, so give it it's due. Here is what a "review" is: *"Our job is to discuss the plan we have, make sure it's doing what it's supposed to do, and check to see if there are changes that require us to reconsider it."* That is a "review." So put that in your script instead of using the one word that turns people off. And don't use its first cousins—"go over" or "look at."

Explain: When you are sitting with someone and they don't understand something you've said, there is nothing wrong with the sentence, "Let me explain it a different way." But without your body language, the word "explain" can sound condescending. Better to avoid it. Here's another word which is better in person: "complicated."

No obligation: Most people don't believe this phrase, so you're better off using other words. Your first appointment is absolutely without obligation, but saying it more effectively would sound like this: *"You can use me, my team, and all the resources at my firm in any way that makes you the most comfortable."*

Death, dying, disability: In the life insurance business, we talk about these things regularly. But they are scary. I cannot imagine why you need to scare people on the first call in order to get an appointment. Essentially, you're trying to get them to accept you as a professional, not sell them something. So there is no need to use these frightening words when setting the appointment. There are a ton of euphemisms for death. Don't use any of them.

Pop in, drop in, stop by: Using these phrases diminish the fact that you live and die by your calendar. You do *not* "pop in" to see people. You schedule agreed-upon times when the prospect can give you 100 percent of their attention. Stay away from these words.

The complete list of Dirty Words is on page 133.

CHAPTER 13

CALLING YOUR FRIENDS & FAMILY

M OST FINANCIAL COMPANIES ASK THEIR NEW ADVISORS to list everyone they know. It is traditionally called Your Project 200, or Your Natural Market. New advisors take the task seriously and write down everyone they know. But then they realize "Hey, I have to *call these people*???"

Sadly, I meet dozens of experienced advisors who have never spoken to their friends and family on a professional basis. When I ask them why, it boils down to the same thing—they didn't think the wording offered by their manager was the right way to talk to these people. Additionally, many of them were given *one* script to use when calling everyone on that 200-plus list. Since the verbiage didn't make sense, they didn't make the calls.

Calling your friends and family can be very difficult. There are three legitimate factors that make these calls intimidating:

First: When you are very close to someone and the relationship is irreplaceable, you don't want a professional call to ruin that relationship. Most of us have one or two really close friends who would be devastated if your call added unnecessary tension to the relationship. And it's not worth the appointment to mess up that unique bond.

Second: If you call someone who is a generation older, it's tricky. Let's face it—people older than you expect to be giving *you* help, not the other way around. It does feel weird to call the parents of your childhood best friend in a professional capacity since they remember you as a young kid. Or your favorite uncle, who is extremely successful and can be a domineering figure. That call can be scary.

Third: If you are calling someone really rich. In general, rich people can be intimidating. When you're a new financial advisor, it feels even more frightening because we bring up the subject of money very directly.

So there are valid reasons to avoid calling the people you know. I get it. But there is an overriding reason to call them. You are in an important profession that can change people's lives for the better. Why would you withhold valuable information from those who mean the most to you?

You need to think differently about your Natural Market.

Everyone you know can be divided among five different categories. Each category represents a different kind of relationship, thereby requiring different language. When I share these categories and the matching scripts, most advisors are relieved. Now the words make sense, and they're willing to make the phone calls.

Here are the five categories:

1. **The very closest people in your world.** That would be your parents, grandparents, siblings, closest friends, and other family members you see often and speak to often. It is *not* the cousins you see at only weddings and funerals.

2. **Friends/acquaintances.** This is the largest group and represents the next level of closeness: the vendors you use (your dry cleaner, mechanic, hairdresser, favorite restaurant owners, etc.); neighbors; buddies with whom you play any sport; people you meet at clubs/organizations; your children's friends' parents.

These folks are not the closest in your life, but they know you and you spend some time with them. For many advisors, this is usually more than half of their list.

3. Anyone you **haven't seen for more than a year.** In normal years, this group would only include former professors, previous co-workers, family you see once or twice a year, former classmates. But due to the pandemic, this group has gotten very large. Perhaps several of your No. 1's and many of your No. 2's are now in this category. For two years, we didn't see many people with whom we normally would have interact. Think carefully about how many from No. 2 really belong here.

4. People who would be more valuable to you as a **Center of Influence (COI)** than a client. That would include influential people in your community, someone who may be "the unelected mayor of your town," a professional person with whom you might want a mutually beneficial cross-referring relationship with or someone, such as a highly influential relative, who can be a phenomenal referral source.

5. Anyone who is **ridiculously rich.** If they are a generation older and you are close to them, that's even more intimidating. You've covered all three factors with that person!

Following is a sample script for each Natural Market category. The first one includes the entire hello and "calling for two reasons." The others do not. In the Scripting section (page 107) there are scripts for experienced advisors, people who have changed financial companies, business owners, etc.

Group No. 1:

"Hi, Grandma, it's me. I'm calling for two reasons. One (ask a personal question). The other reason for my call is that I

wanted to let you know that I started a career as (an agent, financial advisor) at (your company) and I decided I am going to build my practice around the people I care about the most. In fact, they asked us to list those people and of course, you were on the top of my list. I'd like to position myself as a financial resource to you and find a time when I can show you the new scope of the work that I do, and then you can use me and all the resources at my disposal in any way that makes you feel the most comfortable. I know you're very busy, but when is the least hectic time I can visit with you—this week or next?"

Group No. 2:

"Hi, this is (your name), and I'm sure that you've heard about my new career with (your company). I'm really excited about it, and the reason I've called is that I would like to position myself—and my team*—as an additional financial resource to you. I'd like to set a time when we could get together so that we can share with you the total scope of the work that we do. That way, you can use me, my team, and the resources of our company any way that makes you feel the most comfortable. With that in mind, what is less hectic—days or evenings?"

Group No. 3:

This is a networking call! Use the information in Chapter 8 to conduct a catch-up conversation. Schedule a Phone Date prior to calling so you have ample time to have a meaningful conversation. Or if

---

* Change the pronouns back to "me" or "I" if you don't work on a team.

you can randomly dial them and they'll pick up, you can use this script to schedule the catch-up call.

> *"Hi, it's (your name), and it's been a while! I'm calling (or texting or emailing) to find a time to get together for lunch or coffee so we can catch up. I'd like to know what you've been doing (how your family is, etc.) and let you know what's been going on with me as well. What's easier for you—this week or next?"*

Group No. 4 :

> *"Hi, this is (your name), and I'm calling you for help with my business. I don't know if you heard that I have joined (your company), and I'm pretty excited about it. I know that you are very successful and I wanted to set a time when I can visit with you and show you our process to get your opinion on it. For the privilege of picking your brain, I'd like to buy you breakfast/lunch. And I know you're busy, so what is the least hectic day for you—earlier or later in the week?"*

Group No. 5:

> *"Hi, this is (your name), and I'm calling you for help with my business. I don't know if you heard that I have joined (your company), and I'm pretty excited about it. I know that you are very successful, and I wanted to set a time when I can visit with you and show you our process to get your opinion on it. For the privilege of picking your brain, I'd like to buy you breakfast/lunch. And I know you're busy, so what is the least hectic day for you—earlier or later in the week?"*

CHAPTER 14

INTRODUCTIONS & REFERRALS

O THER THAN KNOWING SOMEONE PERSONALLY, your best sources of prospects are referrals and introductions from your clients and friends. Referrals make the world go round. The new challenge is that you can no longer request a phone number and then make a call. The new person probably won't pick up. Therefore, you need help from your referring client to get in touch with the new person.

I do not teach how to ask for referrals. That is the skill of my friend and colleague Bill Cates, the Referral Coach. (See *Resources* on page 135) My job is to help you get in touch with the new person once you have a name.

You need to directly ask your client to help you. Do not make a huge story out of this. Simply say:

> *"Bob, I appreciate your confidence in my work and introducing me to your brother. You know that if I try to call Jason, he will most likely not pick up the phone, so I need your help. I'd like you to send him my contact in a text*, and just tell him three things. One: that you are my client, I'm*

---

* This assumes you are in your client's phone as a Contact (See chapter 4.)

your advisor, and you're happy with the work we've done.
Two: remind him to save the contact, and Three: to take my
call."

Please practice saying the preceding short script. I've role played this with some of my groups, and I hear long-winded stories about why you need help. Everyone is aware that an unknown phone number doesn't get picked up. Keep your request short.

What do you do if they refuse to help you? Maybe they agree to give you a name and number but will not do the rest of the process. Here's how it might play out:

1.   They don't know how to share a contact via text. Often you will be handed their smartphone with the comment, "You do it." This is not a problem unless you have no idea how to use a smartphone that is not the same as yours.

2.   They can't figure out the exact words to say in the text. Not a problem. Just dictate my suggested text below.

3.   They give you a name and number but will not do anything else to help you.

4.   This is a business client and they do not text their colleagues. They use email.

Here is the texted content to dictate to your client:

"I'm extremely happy with my financial advisor, (your
name). He has given me great ideas for my business. I've
attached his contact information. Make sure you save it
in your phone. I told him to call you. Take his call, it will
be worth it."

The easy way to remember the three ideas are:

You want a RAVE (i.e., specific details of your brilliance).

You want a SAVE (keep his/her number).

You want a PICKUP.

Let's solve Problem 3: They will only give you the referral's contact information.

Ask your client for the new person's phone number and email address. Then ask the new person's preferred way of communicating. If it's texting, then you can send a text that says who you are and the person you know in common:

> **"John Smith suggested I reach out to you. I am his financial advisor, and John thought that some of the ideas I shared with him would be of interest to you as well. Please keep my contact information and send me some times you're available for a brief call in the next couple of weeks."**

OR

> **"John Smith thinks you and I should know each other. I usually do whatever John says, so send me some times you're available for a brief call in the next two weeks."**

These may or may not work. Some people resent getting a text from a stranger, even if the first words in your text are the name of a friend.

Let's talk about Problem No. 4: Introduction by email.

Your client might give permission to use their name in an email introduction. That is not as effective as having your client write the email, but you have to follow your client's instructions.

The format for this communication is as follows:

TO: The New Referral

TO: Your Client (Keep the referring person in the loop.)

Subject Line: Introduction from (Client's Name)

The content of the email is similar to the text above.

"John Smith suggested I contact you. I am his financial advisor and John thought that some of the ideas I shared with him would be of interest to you as well. Send me some times you're available for a brief call in the next couple of weeks."

The *better idea* is to ask your client to compose their own email to both you and their friend, writing something about each of you to the other. I have done this type of email introduction, and it takes time and some thought. You want a glowing paragraph about each of the people being introduced. You can only hope that your client will do this for you in the manner below:

The email is written

TO: Their Client (your new introduction)

TO: You

Subject line: Introduction

The content of the email is a paragraph to the client about you, and a paragraph to you about the client. Here is an example of a good email introduction. Your client is John, his client (the introduction) is Richard Shaw, and you are Jane Brown, the agent.

TO: Richard Shaw

TO: Jane Brown

RE: Introduction

"Richard: Jane is my financial advisor and has done a terrific job for me. She's brought some intriguing concepts and ideas to my business and is super smart. I feel very comfortable with her and I think you will, too. She is worth a conversation by phone, at the minimum. I highly recommend her."

"Jane: Richard and I started our businesses at the same time. We are close friends, and he knows my business well—and vice versa. I think he would be a good match for you since you are a straight shooter and helped me a lot. He will appreciate your directness and intelligence."

"Enjoy, John."

Once you know the email has been sent, you immediately write to the new prospect, and hit "Reply All" so your client sees what you are writing.

"Richard,

"John speaks highly of your business and the close relationship you share. I look forward to learning more about how you developed your company. Send me some times you're available in the next two weeks for a brief phone call."

Your full professional signature

Getting introductions is a critical skill for growing your financial practice or your property and casualty business. Through your relationship to another person—a client, friend, relative, etc.—you gain credibility before meeting the new person. Learn how to ask for introductions and your practice will grow.

CHAPTER 15

SPECIALTIES: P&C, HEALTH INSURANCE & 403B MARKET

M Y TRAINING PRACTICE INCLUDES A VARIETY of financial professionals who are specialists. The major content of this book applies to these specialties, but there are still some unique factors to their work.

PROPERTY & CASUALTY AGENTS

Inheriting a Book of Customers

This group often has the gift of many clients at the start. Most of the P&C companies I work with will give a retired agent's book of business to a new agent. That is amazing, since the new agent begins their practice with a vast number of customers.

The biggest job for any new agent is to call everyone to immediately introduce themselves. This can be daunting, but there are ways to organize the names to feel less overwhelmed. Each agent needs to divide the list among the team members. Using the alphabet system (i.e., everyone takes a letter) has worked well for those who inherit this huge opportunity.

The suggested script is similar to the one used by financial advisors who call "Orphan Clients." Most important is to maintain a smiling, friendly tone of voice. The customers usually are happy to hear from you. Sometimes, they are upset to have "lost their agent." You need to be prepared for that.

My favorite wording is humorous. If you can't pull this off, it absolutely won't work. But if you can embrace the silliness, it works like a charm most of the time.

> *"Hello, this is (your name) with (your company) here in (town/location). The reason I am calling is that your agent (name of previous agent) has (retired/is no longer with the company). I'm pleased to tell you that we have inherited each other!"(Giggle a little here. If they laugh too, that's great.)*

> *"I will be your new agent—but right now we have a problem. You are a name on my computer screen, and I'm a strange voice over the phone. I can't possibly do the best job for you without knowing you, so I'd like to schedule a time for us to meet so I can put a face to the name, and you can do the same thing." (Ask for the appointment.)*

> *Alternate Script*

> *"Hello, this is (your name) calling from (your company), here in (town/location). The reason for my call is to personally introduce myself as your new (your company) agent. As you may know, your business was recently transferred to me.** What I would like to do is to set up an appointment to meet face-to-face so that I can share with you how my office can continue the tradition of excellent service that you are used to getting from (your company)."*

** If you know the name of retired agent, you can insert that here.

(Ask for the appointment.)

Client Reviews

The hardest call to make as a P&C Agent is for a homeowner review. The problem is that you keep offering these poor people an appointment to do something that has absolutely no meaning to them. *You have to let go of the word "review."* The *process* of a review is too important to reduce it to one word. And clients don't like the word. So stop using it.

A review is actually a viable, important conversation. Most of my P&C agents tell me that their customers often say, *"I'm not interested"* or *"We just did that"* and don't schedule the appointment. Try using more words! Tell them exactly what happens on this appointment so they understand why they *do* need to discuss their homeowner's policy.

After you say hello, identify yourself and do the "Two reasons for my call." You will get better results with this verbiage:

> *"Hi, Mrs. Smith, this is (your name) calling from (your company) office. I'm calling for two reasons. First, I hope your grandson's graduation from high school was a great event for all of you. (Let them talk a few minutes.). The other reason for my call is that from time to time, our job—you and me—is to discuss the plan we have, make sure it's doing what it's supposed to do, and check to see if there are any changes that require us to reconsider it. What I'd like to do is schedule a time when we can sit together and make sure that everything we are focused on—protecting your house, your car, your possessions and yourself—are all in order. We can do this either virtually, by phone, or in person. Which is best for you?"*

I also recommend that your agency adopt the concept of scheduling Phone Dates. If you send out emails to your customers, you will likely get a high percentage agreeing to a phone call at a time that works for them. Most of my agencies are just randomly dialing and not getting great results. Remember the definition of insanity.

No matter how great you are at taking care of your book of business, you will lose about 10 percent of your customers every year due to no fault of your own. You cannot stand still and only service your clients. Remember to ask for introductions. Unfortunately, introductions are not part of the everyday activities of many property and casualty agencies. Make it a standard part of yours.

Marketing your Property and Casualty Agency

I have already listed several marketing ideas that are great for P&C Agents (see page 42). Your agencies are community-based. Become the "Go To" place for family-focused events that are fun.

Consider every month that has a holiday and plan a community event around that holiday. It's not that hard to schedule an Easter egg hunt in a local park. You have to assign someone on your team to come up with these ideas and strategize on how to execute them smoothly. Doing "Photos With Santa" for free, at your agency, is another fantastic idea. And remember to always invite your clients to bring friends with children. This is how you get known in your community. Offer fun activities and they will come. Every parent with young children is looking for ideas for entertaining family activities. If you solve this problem every other month (or every month if possible) you will get a lot of favorable reviews.

These ideas will not create new clients immediately. But over time, when your clients are introducing you to the same families over and over, you get in a better position to ask them for an appointment. Refer to Chapter 8 on Networking before talking to people at these events.

As the Agent, you should be attending networking events. Don't get discouraged if you see your competition there. People you interact with personally will remember you and be more likely to grant you an appointment. Or they will proactively call you when they need you. But if you're not *there*, they don't know you.

I strongly advise my P&C Agents to consider hiring an Appointment Setter for their team. I have visited busy agencies and they resemble Grand Central Station. There are lot of phones ringing, people rushing around, etc. The office is a busy, busy place. And yet, you have to keep proactively making outbound calls in this environment. Not easy. An employee who *only* does the outbound call is more likely to be less distracted by the other things going on.

Hire an Appointment Setter

Hiring an exclusive appointment setter works for this specific group in a unique way, starting with giving you an in-office solution to scenarios like the three described below:

1. Your staff has a challenging time finding the time to make the outbound calls because of the inbound phone activity.

2. It is difficult to physically isolate a staff person (i.e., put them in another room) so they can concentrate. Calling in the midst of in– and outbound calls is hard. The distraction and disruption level is remarkably high.

3. A ringing phone is hard to ignore. Even if someone is *supposed* to be outbound calling, they see the flashing lights of ignored calls and can't concentrate on what they're doing. They empathize with their overwhelmed colleagues.

Hire someone who is not trained on any of your products or service activities. This person is *solely* an appointment setter. There is a cost to having this person on your team, but I will easily defend why you should hire them. First, they can't get distracted because they don't do the other tasks (like answering the phone). Second, they don't segue into a sale on the phone because they don't know how. They set "pure" appointments each time. Third, they are taught only the language you suggest, so they tend to be more compliant in using the scripts and response handlers.

Let me show you the way to compensate an appointment setter so you know what the "cost" of an appointment setter will be. Assuming they work twenty hours a week and you need twenty confirmed appointments per week, here is the payment schedule:

Appointment Setter Compensation

The appointment setter works a 20-hour week.

They are paid an hourly wage *plus* a bonus for every appointment over the "base number" and every confirmed appointment. A detailed example:

Let's say you pay this person $10/hour. (This might be too low for your area, but I'll upgrade it later.) For their salary, they owe you 5 unconfirmed appointments per week (base appointments).

Their weekly salary is $200. If they set anything over the 5 base appointments, they get a bonus. Any appointments that confirms, they get a bonus.

The first 5 (unconfirmed) appointments they owe you.

The next 3 appointments (Nos. 6, 7, 8) they get $3 for each of those.

The next 3 appointments (Nos. 9, 10, 11) they get $6 each.

The next 3 appointments (Nos. 12, 13, 14) they get $9 each.

The next 3 appointments (Nos. 15, 16, 17) they get $10 each.

Anything over 17 unconfirmed appointments in a week gets

$11 each.

For all appointments that confirm, they get another $3 each.

Here is an example of what 20 confirmed appointments looks like:

1, 2, 3, 4, 5 were covered by the base salary ($200).

Nos. 6, 7, and 8 were $3 each ($9).

Nos. 9, 10, 11 were $6 each ($18).

Nos. 12, 13, 14 were $9 each ($27).

Nos. 15, 16, 17 were $10 each ($30).

The last three were $11 each ($33).

So for 20 unconfirmed appointments you paid the appointment setter $317.

If they all confirmed (20 x $3 = $60) You paid them a *total of* $377.

That's a bargain for 20 confirmed appointments.

So if you look at this pay scale and say, "That won't fly where I live" I can convert the hourly pay to $15/hour and the bonuses are a bit higher as well. The first 5 appointments cost you $300, then the next three (Nos. 6, 7, 8) are $5 each, the following three (9, 10, 11) are $7 each, Nos. 12-14 are $10 each and 15-17 are $12 each. Anything over 17 is paid $15 each. Confirmed appointments are paid at $5 each.

The same 20 confirmed appointments in your market can cost you $547. Again, still a bargain!

I prefer an appointment setter to be someone local. You can, of course, advertise, but it's best if you can get referred. A phone caller works best in a room alone with a phone. But being in the middle of the office, they won't have the same distraction level. Their only job is to outbound call.

Some P&C companies have arrangements with outside telemarketing firms. I get good feedback from some Agents; others tell me the appointments are terrible. I am a controlling person with my own business, so the last thing I would to do is give control of setting my appointments to someone I don't know and who I can't see or hear on the phone.

Yes, it's time consuming to get this appointment setter on board and functioning. But they can become a critical part of your success if they are scheduling new appointments every week.

HEALTH INSURANCE

The health insurance field is unique. Like P&C, it is an "on demand" product. Americans need to have health insurance, which changes your relationship to the customer. Many of my health insurance specialists rely on internet leads as a good source for prospects. The health insurance phone call is unique. First of all, you are following up on a request for specific information. Second, your prospect needs to be qualified—i.e., you need to ask them financial and health questions before making recommendations. Third, you have one shot at the internet prospect because many other agents are reaching out to them. Competition is fierce.

Most of my health insurance agents have their questions at the ready. Some send out a questionnaire immediately if the lead provides an email address. If you can get the prospect on the phone, engagement is the name of the game.

Some health insurance agents prefer to have a conversation with the prospect before getting down to details. These agents believe that creating a warmer relationship will give them a better chance of securing this person's business. Other agents want to be efficient and get down to qualifying questions so the prospect knows they are knowledgeable and ready to help them. Either philosophy works. However, if you are dealing with a referral, someone you know personally or people who have attended a seminar you or your company provided, your phone approach will be different.

Health insurance agents need to form professional alliances with other professionals who do not sell this product. Most of the financial advisors I know want someone dependable to refer their clients to for this necessary product. Health insurance agents need to engage in their community with other professionals, but I find they often don't go to meetings. If your concern is the networking conversation, please go back and read chapter 8. It will work if you use the same technique while speaking with a financial advisor and find out if they need a professional such as yourself.

My coaching sessions with health insurance agents focus on perfecting various aspects of their process. First is the initial engagement, often by text. The primary rule is "Shorter is better."

Let's say you've received a request for a quote from an internet service. Below are six brief text options to send to a prospect. Always attach your Digital Business Card.

1. **"Hi, (prospect name). I recently received your online request for health insurance. When would you have 2-3 minutes to speak so we can compare the options?"**

2. **"I understand that you are looking for health coverage, and I would like the opportunity to see if I can show you a customized a plan to fit your needs and budget."**

3. **"Hello, this is (your name) with (your company). I have a note that you were inquiring about health coverage options. When would you like to set up a time so I can provide you quotes?"**

4. "You were recently online looking for health insurance options. You're probably getting a lot of phone calls, but if you haven't gotten the information you need, please give me a call or let me know when you're available to talk. It will take 2-3 minutes to know if I have what you're looking for."

5. "Hi, (prospect name). I received a note that someone reached out to you recently about health insurance, and you may have expressed an interest in getting a quote. When would you have 2-3 minutes to speak, so I can see if I can help and provide you the info?"

6. "I have the ability to shop all of the health plans that are available to you, but first I want to find out what is important to you. Call me or text."

If a phone number for the prospect is provided, you need two scripts. One for when the person picks up, the other is for a voicemail.

If the prospect picks up:

"Hi, this is (your name), and I am a licensed insurance agent with (your company) here in (your location). Your name was forwarded to me from (website) because you are interested in health insurance. I would like to work with you and make sure you have the information you need to make a good decision. If you have a few minutes now, we can get started." (If they say no: "Generally, what is less hectic for you—daytime or evening?")

"Hi, this is (your name) with (your company), and I'm following up on a request you had over the internet for health insurance, and since I share this information on a face-to-face basis only, the purpose of my call today is to simply find

a mutually convenient time for us to get together and talk about your options. We can do this virtually or in person. Which is better?" (Try to engage them to do it now.)

"Hi, this is (your name) and I am a licensed insurance agent with (your company). Your name was forwarded to me from my company because you've expressed an interest in health insurance. I would like to work with you on finding the best program for your needs, so we need three minutes on the phone so I can assess your situation and give you some numbers. That way, we can get you started on making a good decision. Is this for you alone or for you and your family?"

Voicemail

"This is (your name), I'm a (your city) area insurance agent with (your company) and I don't know if this is a mistake or not, but I'm calling about an online quote request I received recently. If you are looking for health insurance and would like to work with someone from the area, you can let me know by contacting me by text or email." (Leave your email address.)

THE 403b MARKET

Some advisors start their careers working in the 403b market. Those I've spent the most time with "approach educators"—elementary, junior, and senior high school teachers, and university professors—who can enhance their retirement with the equivalent of a 401k. For teachers—and some health professionals—this program is a 403b.

Most of the time, the advisors are granted special permission to visit the teachers in their schools. Obviously, the pandemic put a snag in that. But now most of the schools are back to in-person classes, and financial specialists are once again allowed into the schools.

The reason this is a fabulous start for a new advisor is that it teaches them how to prospect in person and conduct efficient financial conversations. Some advisors are able to meet their teachers in the lounge, where they have the opportunity to casually meet other teachers. Sometimes the advisor is permitted to arrange a group meeting and present the information to a group. But most of the time, the meetings are one-on-one.

The challenge is getting teachers on the phone to schedule an appointment. As with other advisors, virtual appointments increased the ability to get an agreement to talk. Teachers work very long hours and are often too overwhelmed to agree to a financial conversation.

The majority of calls to teachers are done without Phone Dates, which means you need to be "on your game" with your script when they pick up. *"I know you're busy, so I'll be brief"* is a great opening sentence after your introduction. Remember to identify your company and the fact that you are *a partner with the county to provide retirement benefit information to the teachers.*

The best scripts include a unique benefit statement. These advisors have the capacity to provide a teacher with a personalized projection of what their retirement income might be, which includes their pension, Social Security, and 403b. Offering that as part of the financial conversation can be compelling.

Asking *"How are you?"* in this circumstance can seem insincere since you are cold calling. The situation does not allow for a standard *"I'm calling for two reasons . . . "* where you ask a personal questions. You need to phrase the "first reason" differently. A good suggestion for Reason One is that you are the approved provider for their school's 403b options. Reason Two is that you've worked with many other teachers in their school. That easily leads to suggesting that you'd like to schedule a time with them as well. Below is a good script. The advisor is making the assumption that their name is familiar due to their work in the school.

This call is to a new teacher:

"Hi, Jane, this is (your name) and my name may be familiar because I'm from the retirement benefits group. Congratulations on your new position at (school name)! I'm sure you're very excited. I know that as a new employee there is a lot of information thrown at you and I'd like to set up a time for us to meet to go over your retirement benefits with (school name). Our meeting will go through all of it thoroughly, which is a good way for you to feel more comfortable with them. I know your schedule is hectic, but when is the best time to meet for a half hour in the next two weeks?" (Alternative close: "I know your schedule is hectic, but we can meet either in the school or virtually when you're home. Which is more convenient for you?")

"Hi, Rebecca, this is (your name) from (your company). We are the approved provider from the county to talk with you about your retirement benefits at (school). You have both your pension and the opportunity to set up a 403b, which is another optional retirement plan I can talk with you about. I'll also give you a projection on what your expected benefits could be at the time of your retirement. I know you're extremely busy, so I've been scheduling either virtual, at home, or in-person meetings at the school during your break time. Which is better for you?"

I know one very successful advisor who has a strict schedule for herself. She makes her calls and does her in-school prospecting before 4 P.M. After that time, she has back-to-back virtual meetings with her teachers. She found this to be the best way to coordinate her own busy schedule with the high demands of overworked teachers.

Getting a teacher's spouse involved can be challenging, but I've pushed my advisors to engage that other decision maker as soon as possible. If you are meeting your teachers in the school, then you will likely not also be engaging the spouse. If you have virtual appointments either after or before school, the spouse is more likely to be available. This is a good habit to incorporate. Another option is to get the spouse included on a summer appointment. Here is a script to use for summertime visits:

"Hi, this is (your name) with (your company). During the school year we met to discuss your retirement program, and at that time I mentioned to you that I'd be calling you toward this part of April (or May or June). In addition to working with you (and your spouse) on maximizing your retirement options, I'd like to also position myself as a financial resource to you and schedule a time to share with you the total scope of the work that I do. That way, you can use me in any way that makes you the most comfortable. Generally, is a day or evening appointment better for you?"

CHAPTER 16
COMPANY-PROVIDED LEADS
(ORPHANS, MENTOR'S CLIENTS, ETC.)

COMPANY UNALIGNED (ORPHAN) CLIENTS

MANY FINANCIAL COMPANIES HAVE LEADS AND PROSPECTS they offer to their advisors. Most common are the "orphans," who are clients who no longer have an assigned professional. They are also referred to as "unaligned." Whatever your company calls them, they are in need of attention. Many of these people have not been spoken to or visited in a long, long time.

Please do not start out your script reminding the client that your company has neglected them. Your primary goal is to re-engage this person. Too often I hear advisors speaking exclusively about the one life insurance product the client owns. That's not the point of the call! If you only focus on one product during the phone call, that will be the only topic the client expects to discuss on the appointment.

To re-engage a client, you need to do a new financial fact find. Most people have a lot of life changes over the course of five years, and many haven't had an appointment in more than a decade. There's a lot to talk about.

First thing you need to mention is that you have been asked to call them. You are an Ambassador for your company. Your demeanor must be relaxed and friendly. I would add that a touch of humor goes a long way with someone who is feeling neglected by your company. If necessary, mention a specific policy as a way of jogging the client's memory around your company. I've had several advisors meet with total confusion when they introduce themselves and their companies. Sometimes the person you are calling is the owner of a policy that was bought when they were a child. Their recollection may be minimal.

My favorite script has a touch of ridiculousness and usually gets the other person laughing when done correctly. You need to giggle at a designated point in the script because the sentence is silly. The script works best when there is genuine humor exhibited by the agent:

> *"Hi, this is (your name) calling from the local office of (your company), and I'm calling with good news! (pause) I'm pleased to tell you that we have inherited each other. (Here is where you laugh.)*

> *"The company has asked me to be your servicing agent, but right now you and I have a problem. You are a name on a computer screen, and I am a strange voice over the phone. I can't do business this way, so I'd like to schedule a time so that we can both put a face to the name. We can do this either virtually or in person. What would be easier for you?"*

More scripts can be found on page 125.

CALLING YOUR MENTOR'S C+D CLIENTS

Sometimes rookies and experienced advisors are paired up for the benefit of both. It is rare for an advisor to be able to keep track of every client they have on a yearly basis, so it makes sense for the experienced advisors to share their "C+D" clients with younger advisors.

There is a real win-win here. The client gets attention, and the newer advisor gets more experience. Oftentimes, the appointments are conducted by both the older and younger agents, thereby extending their training. Some experienced advisors take on younger ones because the newer advisor is able to do these appointments on their own. These clients are similar to the "orphan" in that they have been overlooked, but in these cases, they belong to an assigned advisor.

As with orphans, do not remind the client of how long it has been since Mr. Experienced Advisor made a call to them. You can reverse that negative concept and make it into a positive right at the beginning of your call.

Here is what I, unfortunately, hear too often: *"Hi, this is Gail Goodman and I'm John Smith's associate. I know it's been a long time since you heard from John . . . "*

Please don't do that.

Here's a better alternative: *"Hi, it's Gail Goodman and I am John Smith's associate. As you know, John doesn't make a lot of unnecessary calls to his clients, but at this junction he SPECIFICALLY asked me to give you a call."*

Remember one specific language rule of these calls: Do not ever say you are "calling on behalf of" the experienced advisor. It makes you sound like you are an assistant, not a licensed professional capable of doing the appointment. You are "the associate" of the older advisor, always!

Here is a script for making these calls:

> ***"Hello, this is (your name) and I am (older agent's name)'s associate. You're probably aware that (older agent) isn't someone who makes unnecessary calls, but at this juncture, he's/she's specifically asked me to call you. From time to time***

it makes sense to sit down with one of us and reassess some of the financial decisions you've made. One thing we know for certain is that things change—either your family situation or the market. I'd like to make sure that the programs you have in place are still working in line with your financial goals. We have three options for you—I can to drive to your house, or you can visit our offices, or we can have a virtual meeting. Which is better for you?"

AGENCY-SPONSORED MARKETING

Agency managers have a variety of ways they provide marketing in your communities. There are two reasons for their efforts: 1. They get the agency noticed by being involved within the community, and 2. They provide prospects for their advisors. Both are great reasons to participate in any program sponsored by the agency. Here are a few of the popular programs:

Financial Literacy Programs

I give a tremendous amount of credit to the dental industry. They have trained all Americans to visit them twice a year. There are few businesses that have created such compliance around what one profession perceives as ideal behavior. They've done a tremendous job.

The financial services industry has not done as much as dentists to increase participation or, ironically, knowledge of their business. One of the best ways to give back to the community and create lifelong financial clients is through Financial Literacy Programs. Some are conducted through large corporations, others through schools and libraries. No matter how your group attacks this huge American problem, embrace any part you are asked to do.

You can also be the catalyst for a financial literacy program without your agency. I know a young woman who became a successful advisor, then went right back to her community to help them rise above their financial challenges through her own newly found knowledge. She boldly approached the principal of her former high school and offered to provide financial literacy classes to the juniors and seniors. They were thrilled at her idea and embraced the suggestion wholeheartedly.

Whether you are part of a group,or do financial training on your own, you will create better citizens and future clients. Your initial call is to the person who can give you access to the attendees. Sometimes it is a corporate officer, other times it is the head of an educational institution. Whichever approach you or your group takes, it is important to stress the benefits of financial knowledge. Here are some examples of calls to those who can give you the green light.

Community Group Reach Out (Call the Executive Director)

"Hi, _____, I've been reaching out to other (insert type of organizations) in (town) to offer a financial wellness program as a service to the community. It's an educational experience, with the goal of helping participants to have better control over their financial life. I'd like to find a time when you have 20–30 minutes so I can show you the curriculum that we've developed. Our research has found that financially educated people are happier and more productive, which is better for the overall community. What is least hectic for you—mornings or afternoons?"

Referral from Someone Who Has Done Your Program

"Hello _____, this is (your name) with (your company) here in (name of town). I was referred to you by (referrer).

He/She thinks very highly of you and your organization and recommended we say hello. My firm conducted a financial literacy program for (referrer) and he/she thought you'd be interested to hear about it. I'd like to find a time to sit down and share the details of the curriculum, which focuses on both individuals and families. In our research, we have found that the lack of financial literacy is wreaking havoc in America today. (Referrer) suggested we get together to see how it fits into your organization. I know you're very busy, but what is less hectic for you, mornings or afternoons?"

Businesses

"Hi, this is (your name), and I am with (your company), and I am calling because our company is providing a free financial literacy program to local businesses. The seminar is designed for large (or small, whichever you're calling) companies who want to provide an educational benefit to their employees, and it's at no cost to you. I would like to schedule a brief meeting to further show you the details of the program. Most employers agree that financially educated and prepared employees means a happier, more productive workforce. In general, what is the least hectic time for you—before or after lunch?"

OR

"Hello, I'm following up on an email I recently sent you regarding our corporate financial planning programs. I work with a lot of benefits coordinators on providing a value-added service to your company, at no charge to you and

with little work on your part. I'd like to set up a mutually convenient time when I can show you the benefits of having corporate-sponsored financial planning seminars for your employees. The win-win arrangement is that we do all the work and you get all the credit."

Agency-Sponsored Seminars

When an agency is sponsoring a seminar, the advisors are asked to invite their clients, friends, and family members. The advisors do not have to create the content, conduct the seminar, find the venue, or get the food. All of that is done for you. The sole responsibility of the advisors is to call people they know and invite them. An effective Seminar Invitation script will share a few specifics:

1. The content is meaningful for that person.

2. There will be a question-and-answer period.

3. There will be refreshments/food/a meal.

4. You will not be the speaker.

5. Other friends can come along.

Managers have expressed disappointment in the attendance of too many sponsored events. They believe the chosen topics are of interest to a specific demographic, but the glitch is in the phone calls and attendance. To improve the attendance, the invitation scripts need to have good wording, and the agents should be using the same language. My best idea is to do a group script. That way, everyone is invested in the language and more likely to actually use it. Group scripting sessions tend to be lively, creative, and fun. The leader of the group will use either a flip chart or white board and start the conversation by vertically writing A, B, C, D, E, F, G. Starting with A, everyone shouts out what they would say for each script component. The most challenging, of course is the D: Why you are calling? Some of the best scripts in this book were written this way. A "group think" script is usually far better than any single agent's script would be.

One word of caution: If you invite your guests to bring along another person who might be interested in the topic, do not give the impression it is a critical feature of their own attendance. One agency realized that the advisors were saying (incorrectly):

"Your price of admission is to bring someone you think would benefit from hearing this information."

That's vastly different from saying: *"Feel free to invite someone, or more than one, to come with you if you think they'd enjoy hearing about this."*

That last sentence ruined the attendance—repeatedly. It took them a while to figure out what was going on when their own friends and clients didn't attend after saying they would. **Remember—every word matters!!**

Here is a good invitation script:

> *"Hi, Aunt Margaret. I'm calling for two reasons. First (ask a personal question that is specific to her life). The other reason for my call is that my firm is sponsoring an interesting workshop, and when I heard about it, I immediately thought of you. It's about (brief description) and I thought you and Uncle John would really want to hear this information. The event is on (date, time, and/or day of the week) and since we are serving a light meal, they've asked us to get an accurate head count. I'd like to save two seats for you."*

CHAPTER 17

PERSISTENT OR A PEST

W E ALL KNOW THAT FOLLOW-UP IS CRITICAL. *How* you follow up—with someone you have met, called, or scheduled an appointment with—is important. You need to be persistent, but you don't want to be a pest. I get asked these questions *a lot*:

How many times do you call someone? How frequently do you follow up if they didn't give you an appointment on the first call? How many times can you request a Phone Date before you're a pest?

You're going to hate me but my answer is—it depends. There are different answers for different situations. One rule of thumb: you don't follow up every day with anyone—ever. You also don't wait several weeks or months unless specifically told to.

The best general advice I can offer is to create a systematic way of following up and stick to it. Unless you get specific instructions from a prospect—"I'll be out of town until next month, so call me the second week in May"—you keep to your system. My system is to wait at least a week, sometimes two, if I am discussing a program with a manager. My clients usually have a team involved in deciding about my programs, so I give them more time than I would if I were an advisor. But a week is reasonable for you.

101

If you have called someone and left a message, you can call them again within four days. If you spoke to someone and they say they need you to call them back at another time, wait a week or ten days. If you don't have enough prospects, you will find it hard to follow my suggestions. Many advisors are calling, emailing, and texting people too often because they don't have enough people to call. The whole purpose of this book is to get you to do more prospecting so you have more people in your pipeline.

Here are some specific situations with detailed follow up plans:

Scenario No. 1: You met someone at a social event, engaged in a great conversation, and exchanged contact information, but you did not get to the point of asking to continue the conversation in another venue. Your next move is to text or email them for a Phone Date.

> **"John, I enjoyed our conversation at Sam and Ellen's barbecue last weekend and wanted to continue it. Let me know some times you're available for a brief call in the next couple of weeks."**

Once you have the Phone Date (and it's confirmed), your phone script would be:

> *"Hi, John, (small talk about event at Sam and Ellen's). I noticed that when we were talking, you had said you were concerned about keeping your most valuable executives at your company without literally tying them to their chairs. I had mentioned that I've worked with other CEOs in the same situation and wanted to find a time to go for either coffee or lunch so I can expand on that with you. What's generally the easier for you, earlier or later in the week?"*

Scenario No. 2: You met someone at a networking event and spoke extensively, but you didn't exchange information, so you're not in their phone. To find this person's contact information, ask the host of the event. Let them know you spent time with the other guest but forgot to get their number. Your message is the same, whether you email or text. Remember that with emails, you need to put in a subject line.

Email Subject Line: (Name of Event)

"Hi, John, I enjoyed our conversation at the Meet 'n Greet event and wanted to continue our conversation. Send me some times you're available for a brief call in the next couple of weeks."

For the phone call, here is your script:

"Hi, John, I'm calling for two reasons: (small talk about event). The other reason for my call is that I noticed that when we were talking, you had said you were concerned about keeping your most valuable executives at your company. I had mentioned that I've worked with other CEOs in the same situation and wanted to find a time to go for either coffee or lunch so I can expand on that with you. What's generally easier for you, earlier or later in the week?"

Scenario No. 3: You have the email and phone number of someone who attended your seminar on retirement ideas. You called them once, but didn't get an answer and left a voicemail. Wait two days, then send them an email.

"Hi, Gail, I'm glad you had an opportunity to attend my seminar on retirement investment ideas. Most of the information is general, which is why I like to reach out to everyone and give them a chance to talk about the specifics—i.e., your personal situation. Send me some times you're available in the next two weeks for a phone call."

Scenario No. 4: You started a conversation with someone at a business networking event, but they had to leave abruptly to introduce the speaker. You didn't get their phone information, but had a long enough discussion to have identified something in their work/personal life to bring up. Send an email with the subject line "Continue our Conversation."

> **"Hi, Robert,**
>
> **"I enjoyed meeting and talking with you at the _____ event on Tuesday. Great speaker. Clearly you two have a long-standing friendship.**
>
> **"I'd like to continue our conversation on the potential sale of your company. I have worked with other business owners in the same situation. Send me some times you're available for a brief call in the next couple of days."**

The phone call should be an invitation to lunch so you can get more information before making any financial suggestions. If a conversation gets stymied, don't work with the small amount of information you acquired. Extend the getting-to-know-you conversation.

NETWORKING QUESTIONS, SCRIPTS & DIRTY WORDS

QUESTIONS TO ASK AT
NETWORKING AND SOCIAL EVENTS

Questions to ask at a Networking (business) Event

Have you been to this event before?

What keeps you coming back?

How did you learn of this event?

Are there other events you attend?

What type of work do you do?

Do you like what you do?

How did you get involved in that field?

What made you change your career path?

What are your goals for the year?

What are your long-range business goals?

How did you survive the pandemic?

How do you market your business?

How do you get most of your business?

Do you have a target market?

Who is a perfect prospect for you?

Who are the best referral sources for you?

Who are you looking to meet here?

How can I help?

Questions to ask at a Social Event

How do you know (host's name)? (Allow this part of the conversation to continue.)

When you're not balancing food and a drink, what do you do?

Do you like what you do?

How did you start your business?

How is business going?

How were you (or your industry) affected by the pandemic?

Why do you think your business survived?

Who are your best clients?

How do you market your business?

How many employees do you have?

Are you looking to grow your business (or are you looking to retire)?

What's the hardest part of your business/industry?

Where is your business heading in the next few years?

How can I help you?

SCRIPTS*

NATURAL MARKET
Group No. 1—For New Advisors

"Hi, this is (your name) and I'm sure that you've heard about my new career with (your company). I'm really excited about it, and the reason I've called is that I would like to position myself—and my team*—as an additional financial resource to you. I'd like to set a time when we could get together so that I can share with you the total scope of the work that we do. That way, you can use me, my expertise, and the resources of our company any way that makes you feel the most comfortable. With that in mind, what is less hectic—earlier or later in the week?"

"I wanted to let you know that I started a career as (an agent, financial advisor) at (your company) and I decided I am going to build my practice around the people I care about the most. In fact, they asked us to list those people and, of course, you were on the top of my list. I'd like to position myself as a financial resource to you and find a time when I can show you the new scope of the work that I do and then you can use me, and all the resources at my disposal, in any way that makes you feel the most comfortable."

---

*If you bring your manager with you on your appointments, using "my team" and the pronoun "we" is important.

"I don't know if you've heard, but I've become involved in a new career that I'm really excited about, and I wanted to call you to share my news. I've joined (your company), and I'm focusing my work on helping the people I know best to address their financial goals. At this juncture, I simply would like to position myself and my team as an additional financial resource to you and spend some time together to show you the total scope of the work that we do. That way you can use me and all the resources we have in any way that makes the most sense to you."

Group No. 1—Experienced Advisors

Apology Script: *"John, I'm so glad I bumped into you because I need to tell you that I owe you an apology. (Pause and let them absorb what you just said.) You know that I have been in financial services for more than _____ years, and in all that time I've never reached out to you on a professional basis, and I need to rectify that. I would like to be an additional financial resource to you, and I want us to get together so that I can share with you the total scope of the work that I do. That way, you will be better able to use my expertise any way that makes you feel the most comfortable. I know you're usually very busy, but when can we go for coffee or lunch?"*

"Hi, it's (your name). I'm calling you because I feel that I have been professionally irresponsible, in that I have never called you and offered you my assistance in my professional

capacity. I would like to position myself as an additional financial resource to you. In order to figure out how to do that, I'd like to get together and share with you the total scope of the work that I do. Then you'll be able to use my experience and knowledge any way you see fit. When can I take you out for a cup of coffee—this week or next?"

Group No. 2—Acquaintances, Friends, Vendors

"Hi, this is (your name), and I'm sure that you've heard about my new career with (your company). I'm really excited about it, and the reason I've called is that I would like to position myself and my team as an additional financial resource to you. I'd like to set a time when we could get together so that we can share with you the total scope of the work that we do. That way, you can use me, my team, and the resources of our company any way that makes you feel the most comfortable. With that in mind, what is less hectic—days or evenings?"

(Change the pronouns back to "me" or "I" if you are experienced and don't work on a team.)

Group No. 3

"Hi, it's (your name) and it's been a while! I'm calling to find a time to get together for lunch or coffee so we can catch up. I'd like to know what you've been doing (how your family is, etc.) and let you know what's been going on with me as well. What's easier for you—this week or next?"

Group No. 4

"Hi, this is (your name) and I'm calling you for help with my business. I don't know if you heard that I have joined (your company), and I'm pretty excited about it. I know that you are very successful, and I wanted to set a time when I can visit with you and show you our process to get your opinion on it. For the privilege of picking your brain, I'd like to buy you breakfast/lunch. And I know you're busy, so what is the least hectic day for you—earlier or later in the week?"

Group No. 5

"Hi, this is (your name) and I'm calling you for help with my business. I don't know if you heard that I have joined (your company) and I'm pretty excited about it. I know that you are very successful and I wanted to set a time when I can visit with you and show you our process to get your opinion on it. For the privilege of picking your brain, I'd like to buy you breakfast/lunch. And I know you're busy so what is the least hectic day for you—earlier or later in the week?"

BUSINESS OWNERS YOU KNOW

"The reason I'm calling is that I've made a career switch to (your company), and I was in a business concepts class the other day and thought of you. They were discussing ideas that can save a small business owner like you important money, enough that it would affect your bottom line. I would like to schedule an appointment to talk to you briefly

about these ideas because if I were able to show you how to save money in your business, I'd certainly like to do that."

"Last week I was sitting with a client with a business just like yours and I thought of you. I wanted to give you a call because in my financial practice my primary focus has been on assisting (professionals and/or) business owners in enhancing their personal (and business) financial position. I'd like to get together and show you some of the ideas I've shared with my other business clients."

RECALLING YOUR NATURAL MARKET

"I was sitting in a class that was primarily about (small businesses, young families saving for college, a subject of interest to them), and I kept thinking of you. I wanted to call and invite you to join me for a cup of coffee so that I can give you some of these really terrific ideas that I learned. I felt that I would be neglecting you if I didn't share them."

OVERHEARING FINANCIAL CONCERNS

"Hi, this is (your name). We recently were at (event), and I overheard you mentioning a concern about (example: paying for college, paying for benefits, the current economy). Because I am a financial professional, I hear those kinds of comments with a different ear, so the reason for my call today is to position myself as an additional financial resource. I'd like to schedule a time when we can sit down and I can show you the total scope of the work that I do, and you

can then decide how you might like to use me and all my resources."

"Hi, this is (your name), and we were at (name of event), and during a discussion you said that you were concerned about _____. As a financial professional, I hear those kinds of comments differently, so it motivated me to call you. I'd like to offer to position myself as an additional resource to you and your family/business and get together so I can show you the total scope of the work that I do. Then you can use me and all my resources any way that feels most comfortable to you."

TRANSITIONING EXPERIENCED ADVISORS

"Hi, this is (your name) (from old company if appropriate). I don't know if you've heard, but I have made a lateral move in my career and I have partnered with a terrific organization (name of organization). I did this because I thought it would be good for me and good for you. I would like to get together with you to show you the new scope of the work that I now do, and I am sure that I will be a more effective financial resource to you in my new capacity."

REFERRALS/INTRODUCTIONS

"Hi, this is (your name) and a friend/ colleague of yours (referring person) suggested that I give you a call. (Referring person) is not only a friend of mine, but she is also my client. I'm with (your company), and we recently met and I

did some very good financial work with (referrer) and she wanted me to call you. All I would like to do at this point is position myself as an additional financial resource to you and schedule a time when I can share with you the total scope of the work that I do. That way, you can use me any way that makes you feel comfortable."

"Hi, this is (your name), and a mutual friend suggested I give you a call. (Friend's name) is both my friend and client, and I am his advisor. Harry speaks very highly of you. I am with (your company) and recently, we met to discuss some ideas for _____, and he thought that some of the concepts I shared with him might interest you. What I'd like to do is get together, show you the total scope of the work I do, and then you can use me in any way that makes you most comfortable."

If a Center of Influence Has Introduced You:

"Hi, this is (your name), and recently, I was with (referrer) and he suggested I give you a call. (Referrer) and I are friends and were talking about our businesses and as a financial professional with (your company), he thought I could position myself as an additional resource to you/your business. I'd like to find a time when we can meet for a cup of coffee and I can share with you the scope of the work that I do, which will allow you to figure out the best way to use both myself and all the resources of my company."

If You Have Been Referred to a Possible Center of Influence:

"Hello, this is (your name), and I was referred to you by (name of referring person) and the reason I was calling is that I am looking for other professionals who can provide complementary services to my clients. I only give my clients high-quality service, and I am looking for other professionals who pride themselves on doing the same thing. (Referrer) thought you were that type of person and told me to call you. So I'm calling to see if I could set up a time for us to get together and discuss the possibility of pooling our resources for the benefit of our potential mutual clients."

Calling a Potential Center of Influence You Know:

"Hi, this is (your name), and I'm calling because in my financial practice I am often in a position to need the services of an attorney/accountant, and I immediately thought of you. What I'd like to do is find a time when we can sit and talk in more detail about our respective practices and see if there is a basis for us to consider doing some introducing to the other's clients."

Calling the Referral from a Center of Influence:

"Hi, this is (your name), and I was recently with (referrer) and he/she suggested that I give you a call. (Referrer) and I are colleagues and frequently find that our clients need the services of the other. That is the reason for my call. I am a financial advisor with (your company), and I work with

people on (financial issue that is appropriate for this client). (Referrer) suggested that we schedule a time to sit down, and I can share with you the scope of the work that I do and see how, along with (referrer), I can be part of your professional team."

TARGET MARKETS

Sample Target Market Language

Here are some examples of scripts for specific groups. The targeted group is underlined but can be changed. They all require you to add a close at the end. Notice some of the language that can be incorporated, both on the phone and in person. Feel free to modify and use some of these for the groups you are pursuing:

"I specialize in working with <u>florists</u> since my family has been in the <u>floral business</u> for forty years and I am familiar with the cyclical nature of the business. I have been able to sit down with other <u>florists</u> and assist in identifying appropriate concepts and ideas to meet either their current goals or future goals."

"As a <u>former restaurant manager</u>, I have focused my current work in the financial services industry on helping my colleagues in the <u>food business</u> to be able to meet their financial goals. What I would like to do is visit with you and briefly discuss some of the financial programs that I think meet the unique needs of <u>restaurant owners</u>. In this short visit, we can get to know each other and then if you think my ideas are helpful, we can take it from there."

"Being a <u>former manufacturer</u>, I have focused my current work in the insurance and investment industry on providing ideas to executives in the <u>garment center</u>. These concepts are designed to help them manage their unique problems associated with cash flow, retirement, and other serious financial challenges. I would like to share some ideas that I think you will find helpful to achieve the financial success you deserve."

"The last time we spoke, as you may recall, I was helping <u>military families</u> build a strong financial future. I am working with (your company) because it gives me the ability to be a financial resource to my friends who aren't in the service. I would love to sit down with you and (his/her spouse) to show you the total scope of the work I'm doing, and then you can decide how to best use all of our resources."

BUSINESS MARKETS

Retirement Specialist—Natural Market

"Hi, _____ , it's (your name). I'm calling for two reasons. (Ask a personal question about their life and let this part of the conversation continue for a couple of minutes.) The other reason for my call is that I haven't spoken to you about the work my firm does for companies with retirement plans. I know you provide such a plan to your employees, and I'd be remiss if I didn't share with you some of the ideas that I've been sharing with business owners who are not my (friends/relatives). The unique approach we have is

that we work from a service-oriented model. We analyze a variety of fees that can easily get expensive for the company. In addition, our goal is to protect the person with the fiduciary responsibility for the plan, making sure they are audit-ready at all times. I'd like to have a face-to-face meeting with you and the other executives who are in charge of your plan. What is least hectic for you, generally, earlier or later in the week?"

For your own clients:**

"Hi, _____ , it's (your name). I'm calling for two reasons. First, I wanted to briefly talk about (product, form, whatever reason you would call them—even a personal one). The other reason for my call is that I recently did some work with a client who has a retirement plan very similar to yours. I have been remiss in not telling you that I have access to a variety of resources to help you with your company plan as well. Without going into a lot of detail, I'd like to schedule a meeting where I can describe the analysis we do on a variety of features of a retirement plan. I know your days are busy, so I'd be happy to schedule a time early in the morning before things get too hectic."

For clients who can refer you within their company:**

"Hi, _____ , it's (your name). I'm calling for two reasons. First, I wanted to briefly talk about (product, form, whatever reason you would call them). The other reason for my call is that I know that at (their company) you are participating in

---

** Remember, if you have a scheduled appointment with this client, this entire script can, and should, be done in person.

the retirement plan. Our firm has an exclusive division that works with the people who are in charge of plans like yours. The way your retirement plan is managed can have an impact on your own portion of it. I would like to speak to the person in charge of your plan, but I would need you to introduce me to them."

CORPORATE NESTING

"Hi, _____ , this is (your name) from (your company). I know you're busy, so I'll be brief. I do a lot of work with (their company) employees in helping them to assess their current benefits package, especially their retirement plan. Most plans only provide an 800 number for employees to get personalized information, or questions answered, and I would like to position myself as an additional financial resource to you as I've done with some of your colleagues. I will be visiting your company next week and would like to meet with you for about fifteen minutes so you can see the total scope of the work that I do."

"Hi, this is (your name), and my name may be familiar to you because I've been working with some of your colleagues at (their company) and speaking to them about the generous benefits package you receive. I'm a financial professional with (your company), and my work focuses on helping people to understand their benefits and, more importantly, see how they fit in with their family's needs. I'd like to find a time when we can meet for about fifteen

minutes, either in person or virtually, and I can show you the total scope of work I do. What is generally the least hectic time in your workday—before or after lunch?"

SOCIAL EVENT FOLLOW-UP
Emailed/Texted for a Phone Date

"Hi, John, (small talk about event at Sam and Ellen's). I noticed that when we were talking, you had said you were concerned about keeping your most valuable executives at your company without literally tying them to their chairs. I had mentioned that I've worked with other CEOs in the same situation and wanted to find a time to go for either coffee or lunch so I can expand on that with you. What's generally the easier for you, earlier or later in the week?"

AGENCY-SPONSORED SEMINAR
Invitation Call

"Hi, Aunt Margaret. I'm calling for two reasons. First (ask a personal question that is specific to her life, not a general "How are you?" which can lead to a tangent). The other reason for my call is that my firm is sponsoring an interesting workshop, and when I heard the topic, I immediately thought of you. It's about (brief description), and I thought you and Uncle John would really want to hear this information. The event is on (day, time, date), and since we are serving a meal, they've asked us to get an accurate head count. I'd like to save two seats for you."

Invited to Seminar—Didn't/Couldn't Attend

"I am following up with those who were unable to attend our (title) seminar and offering to get together with you to discuss some of the highlights of the program. If we can schedule a time—either in person or virtually—I can give you an abbreviated version of the program, and personalize it to your situation."

ADVISOR SEMINARS

Invitation Call

"I'm calling you to follow up on the invitation I sent about the workshop on (topic) on (date). I think you and ___ would find it very valuable. We will be bringing in our retirement planning specialist to speak, and I'm confident a lot of interesting information will be shared. We also want to keep the group to a size that allows for an interactive conversation. Since we are serving a dinner, we need an accurate head count. Can I reserve two seats for you and _____ on the evening of (date)?"

Invitation Follow-up for Client Invitation:

"Hello, this is (your name) with (your company). I'm calling to follow up on an invitation we sent you to our upcoming seminar on (date). Many of my clients have expressed a concern and interest in this topic so, I've decided to offer more information in a public arena. I think this topic is one that relates to several of OUR conversations. I'm keeping the seating limited so the group is small enough for questions.

How many seats would you like us to save for you?"

After Seminar—Expressed Interest in an Appointment:

"Hello, this is (your name). At our seminar on (date) you indicated that you were interested in a private consultation/appointment so we can personalize the information for you. I'd be happy to visit with you to do that. What is the easiest way to meet—virtually? Or my office?"

Invited to Seminar—Didn't/Couldn't Attend:

"I am following up with those who were unable to attend our (title) seminar and offering to get together with you to discuss some of the highlights of the program. If we can schedule a time—either virtually or my office—I can give you an abbreviated version of the program, and personalize it to your situation."

TRADE SHOW FOLLOW-UP

"Hi, John, it's (your name). We met briefly at the (trade show) but didn't have enough time to really find out more about each other's business. I'd like to continue our conversation and wanted to find out what would be the best time for coffee. I'd be happy to meet you at the closest Starbucks, or if your week is hectic, I can bring you some caffeine when you need it. Which one sounds better?"

REFERRALS

Introduction Text Was Sent by Referrer:

"Hi, this is (your name). Good to meet you on the phone, and John speaks very highly of you. (Appropriate social conversation about the referring person.) I'd like to schedule a time to share with you the total scope of the financial work that I do, and then you can see why (John) suggested that we meet. I meet with people in person, but we can also schedule a virtual meeting. Which is better for you?"

***Not* Introduced by a Referrer:**

"Hi, this is (your name), and a friend/colleague of yours (referrer), suggested that I give you a call. (Referring person) is not only a friend of mine, but she is also my client. I'm with (your company), and we recently met and I did some very good financial work with (referrer) and she wanted me to call you. All I would like to do at this point is position myself as an additional financial resource to you and schedule a time when I can share with you the total scope of the work that I do. That way, you can use me any way that makes you feel comfortable."

"Hi, this is (your name), and a mutual friend suggested I give you a call. Harry Smith is both my friend and client and I am his financial advisor—and he speaks very highly of you. I am with (your company), and recently,we met to discuss some ideas for (himself, his employees, whatever works here), and he thought that some of the concepts I

shared with him might interest you. What I'd like to do is get together, show you the total scope of the work I do, and then you can use me in any way that makes you most comfortable."

If a Center of Influence Has Introduced You:

"Hi, this is (your name), and recently I was with (COI) and he suggested I give you a call. (COI) and I are friends and were talking about our businesses and as a financial professional with (your company). He thought I could position myself as an additional financial resource to you/your business. I'd like to find a time when we can meet for a cup of coffee, either in person or virtually, and I can share with you the scope of the work that I do. Then you can figure out the best way to use both myself and all the resources of my company."

If You Have Been Referred to a Possible Center of Influence:

"Hello, this is (your name), and I was referred to you by (referrer) and the reason I was calling is that I am looking for other professionals who can provide complementary services to my clients. I only give my clients Cadillac service, and I am looking for other professionals who pride themselves on doing the same thing. (Referrer) thought you were that type of person and told me to call you. So I'd like to set up a time for us to get together and discuss the possibility of pooling our resources for the benefit of our potential mutual clients."

Calling a Potential Center of Influence You Know:

"Hi, this is (your name), and I'm calling because in my financial practice I am often in a position to need the services of an attorney/accountant, and I immediately thought of you. What I'd like to do is find a time when we can sit and talk in more detail about our respective practices, show you the process I use with clients, and see if there is a basis for us to consider doing some referring to the other's clients."

Hi, this is (your name), and I'm calling you for help with my business. I don't know if you heard that I have joined (your company), and I'm pretty excited about it. I know that you are very successful, and I wanted to set a time when I can visit with you and show you our process to get your opinion on it. For the privilege of picking your brain, I'd like to buy you breakfast/lunch. And I know you're busy, so what is the least hectic day for you—earlier or later in the week?"

Calling the Referral from a Center of Influence:
(Make sure the COI sent your contact information first.)

"Hi, this is (your name) and I was recently with (COI) and he/she suggested that I give you a call. (COI) and I are colleagues and frequently will find that our clients need the services of the other. That is the reason for my call. I am a financial advisor with (your company), and I work with people on (financial issue that is appropriate for this client.) (COI) suggested that we schedule a time to sit down, and I can share with you the scope of the work that I do and see how, along with (COI), I can be part of your professional team."

ORPHAN CALLS

"Hi, this is (your name)calling from the local office of (your company), and I'm calling with good news! (pause) I'm pleased to tell you that we have inherited each other.*** The company has asked me to be your servicing agent, but right now you and I have a problem. You are a name on a computer screen and I am a strange voice over the phone. I can't do business this way, so I'd like to buy you a cup of coffee so that we can both put a face to the name. What would be easier for you—meeting at a Starbucks or your home? Or, if you prefer, we can do this meeting virtually."

"I'm calling with great news! (pause) We have inherited each other.*** However, you and I have a problem. Right now, you are a name on a manila folder, and I am a strange voice over the phone. Right now, I wouldn't even recognize you if we were to bump into each other at the grocery store. So I'd like to schedule a time when we can get together so we can both put a face to the name and be more comfortable with each other." (close)

"Good morning, this is (your name) from (your company). I'm calling for two reasons; the first is to say thank you for being a loyal client for so long, and the second is introduce myself as your local advisor here in (your city or town). Our company has played a little bit of matchmaker here, and I want to see if we can make the relationship work. (your ompany) has multiple resources that you have access

---

*** Here is where you laugh.

to, and I personally want you to benefit from. As an advisor, I want to complete a health check of your policy as well as share the full scope of our resources pertinent to you. I also want to be able to put a face to the name and for you to do the same. Is there a general time of the week or during the day that is best for you? We can schedule either an in-person or virtual conversation—whatever you are most comfortable with."

"Hi, _____. This is (your name). I am one of your local (your company) financial professionals. I'm calling you for two reasons, and I will be very brief. One, I want to take a moment to thank you for continuing to allow (your company) to have such an important role in your and your family's life. The other reason for my call is that I'd like to introduce myself as your new contact for service for your existing plans with (your company) as well as to make you aware of additional services that you are eligible for as a longtime client in good standing. Most importantly, I'd like to learn more about you and ways that you feel both I and (your company) can be a better resource to you. When are you available for a virtual cup of coffee? Earlier or later in the day?"

Staff Person Call to Orphan Client:

"Hi, _____, this is (your name) I work with (agent) at (your company) in (city/town). I have good news! We have inherited each other. (Pause.) The company has asked

(agent) to be your servicing agent. We would like to give you the best service possible, but right now we can't do that when you are just a name on a computer screen to us, and we are a strange voice over the phone to you. _____ would like to schedule a time when you can meet—maybe for a cup of coffee, so that you can both put a face to the name."

CALLING YOUR MENTOR'S C+D CLIENTS

"Hello, this is (your name) and I am (older agent's name)'s associate. You probably are aware that (older agent) isn't someone who makes unnecessary calls, but at this juncture, he's/she's asked me to call you. From time to time it makes sense to sit down with one of us and reassess some of the financial decisions you've made. One thing we know for certain is that things change—either your family situation or the market. I'd like to make sure that the programs you have in place are still working in line with your financial goals. I'm happy to drive to your house or you are always invited to visit our offices. Which is better for you?"

FINANCIAL LITERACY PROGRAMS
Community Group Reach Out

"Hi, _____, I've been reaching out to other (insert type of organizations) in (town) to offer a financial wellness program as a service to the community. It's an educational experience, with the goal of helping the participants to have better control over their financial life. I'd like to find a time

where you have 20 to 30 minutes so I can show you the curriculum that we've developed. Our research has found that financially educated people are happier and more productive, which is better for the overall community. What is least hectic for you—mornings or afternoons?"

Referral from Another Literacy Program Client:

"Hello, _____, this is (your name) with (your company) here in (town). I was referred to you by _____. He/She thinks very highly of you and your organization, and recommended we get to say hello. Our firm conducted a financial literacy program for (referrer), and he/she thought you'd be interested to hear about it. I'd like to find a time to sit down and share the details of the curriculum, which focuses on both individuals and families. In our research, we have found that the lack of financial literacy is wreaking havoc in America today. (Referrer) suggested we get together to see how it fits into your organization. I know you're very busy, but what is less hectic for you, mornings or afternoons?"

Business Owner (or Benefits Director):

"Hi, this is (your name), and I am with (your company), and I am calling because our company is providing a free financial literacy program to local businesses. The seminar is designed for large (or small, whichever you're calling) companies who want to provide an educational benefit to their employees, and it's at no cost to you. I would like to schedule a brief meeting to further show you the details of

the program. Most employers would agree that financially educated and prepared employees mean a happier, more productive workforce. In general, what is the least hectic time for you—before or after lunch?"

"I'm following up on an email I recently sent you regarding our corporate financial planning programs. I work with a lot of benefits coordinators on providing a value-added service to your company, at no charge to you and with little work on your part. I'd like to set up a mutually convenient time when I can show you the benefits of having corporate-sponsored financial planning seminars for your employees. The win-win arrangement is that we do all the work and you get all the credit."

CONGREGATION LEADER

"Hello, _____, this is (your name) I wanted to speak to you about setting up a time when we can discuss my helping our church/temple with an improved charitable giving program. There are several ways it can be set it up so that the outcome is a clear win-win situation—there is more money for our congregation, but there are significant tax benefits to the giver. These programs have been very successful in other churches/temples, and I'd like to see ours get the same increase in generous donations."

RETIREMENT PLANNING SPECIALIST

Business Clients:

> *"Hi, _____, it's me. I'm calling for two reasons. (Ask a personal question about their life and let this part of the conversation continue for a couple of minutes.) The other reason for my call is that I haven't spoken to you on a professional basis about the work my firm does for companies with retirement plans. I know you provide such a plan to your employees, and I'd be remiss if I didn't share with you some of the services and ideas that I've been sharing with people that are not my clients. The unique approach we have is that we work from a service-oriented model. First, we analyze a variety of fees that can easily get expensive for the company. Second, our goal is to protect the person with the fiduciary responsibility for the plan, making sure they are audit-ready at all times. I'd like to have a face-to-face meeting with you and the other executives that are in charge of your plan. What is least hectic for you—generally—earlier or later in the week?"*

> *"Hi, _____, it's (your name). I'm calling for two reasons. First, I wanted to briefly talk about (product, form, whatever reason you would call them—even a personal one). The other reason for my call is that I recently did some work with a client who has a retirement plan very similar to yours. I have been remiss in not telling you that I have access to a variety of resources to help you with your company plan as well. Without going into a lot of detail on the phone, I'd like*

130

to schedule a meeting where I can describe the analysis we do on a variety of features of a retirement plan. I know your days are busy so I'd be happy to schedule a time early in the morning before things get too hectic."

For Clients Who Can Refer You to Their Employer:

"Hi, _____, it's (your name). I'm calling for two reasons. First, I wanted to briefly talk about (product, form, whatever reason you would call them). The other reason for my call is that I know that at (their company) you are participating in the retirement plan. Our firm has an exclusive division that works with the people who are in charge of plans like yours. The way your retirement plan is managed can have an impact on your own portion of it. I would like to speak to the person in charge of your plan, but I would need you to introduce me to them."

CORPORATE NESTING: ZOOM INFO LEADS

"I do a lot of work with (their company) employees in helping them to assess their current benefits package, especially their retirement plan. Most plans only provide an 800 number for employees to get personalized information, and I would like to position myself as an additional financial resource to you as I've done with some of your colleagues. I will be visiting your company next week and would like to meet with you for about fifteen minutes so you can see the total scope of the work that I do."

"Hi, this is (your name), and my name may be familiar to you because I've been working with some of your colleagues at (their company) and speaking to them about the generous benefit package you receive. I'm a financial professional with (your company) and my work focuses on helping people to understand their benefits and, more importantly, see how they fit in with their family's needs. I'd like to find a time when we can meet for about fifteen minutes, and I can show you the total scope of work I do and be an additional financial resource to you. What is generally the least hectic time in your workday—before or after lunch?"

ASSOCIATION MEMBER

"Hello, Mr./Mrs. Business, this is (your name) calling from (your company). Our name is probably familiar to you because we have an alliance with (association) and are the approved provider for different benefits for the members. You have probably seen the letter from (association) announcing this relationship. I'd like to find a time when the two of us can sit down, and I will show you the scope of the work that we do for (association)'s business owners, and you can see how we're sharing creative ideas for their benefits program. What is the easiest time for us to spend minutes—earlier or later in the day?"

DIRTY WORDS

Review
Go over
Look at
Hook up
Explain
Free
No-obligation
Eplain
Present
Verify
Update
Teach
Introduce
Tell you
Help (you)
Complicated
Solution
Life insurance
Die
Death
Disability
Demise
Croak
Kick the bucket
Pass over transition
God forbid
Tragedy
Pop-in
Drop-in
Stop by
In the area

RESOURCES

Michael Goldberg—www.knockoutnetworking.com

Bill Cates—www.referralcoach.com

ABOUT THE AUTHOR

When YOU HEAR THE NAME "THE PHONETEACHER," that refers to Gail B. Goodman. She has spent more than three decades teaching financial advisors, insurance agents, managers, and trainers how to schedule appointments with new prospects.

Ms. Goodman's training has been updated to respond to our ever-changing world. However, the pandemic created a new set of challenges and changes, which are addressed in this, her newest book.

Along with technology, our language evolves. Old ways of speaking to prospects, asking for appointments, and listening to their responses will not work for the modern financial advisor.

Ms. Goodman is also the author of *Modern Appointment Setting—Prospecting and Phoning for Financial Professionals*.

Ms. Goodman lives on a horse farm outside of Nashville with her husband and too many animals.

www.ingramcontent.com/pod-product-compliance
Lightning Source LLC
Chambersburg PA
CBHW031942190326
41519CB00007B/630